God's Intentions for Mankind

Armand J. Horta

To Raymond
My God Bless
Armand J. Horta

Note for Librarians: A cataloguing record for this book is available from Library
and Archives Canada at www.collectionscanada.ca/amicus/index-e.html

Printed in Victoria, BC, Canada.

ISBN: 978-1-4269-1415-7 (sc)

Trafford rev. 09/4/09

 www.trafford.com

North America & international
toll-free: 1 888 232 4444 (USA & Canada)
phone: 250 383 6864 ♦ fax: 250 383 6804 ♦ email: info@trafford.com

The United Kingdom & Europe
phone: +44 (0)1865 487 395 ♦ local rate: 0845 230 9601
facsimile: +44 (0)1865 481 507 ♦ email: info.uk@trafford.com

TO ALL RELIGIONS

Please read the entire book, all of the most popular religions and their basic teachings are mentioned and taught throughout the chapters. Do not become discouraged because of the reference to Jesus. Jesus did not want to start a religion. He wanted to teach everyone a way of life and path toward God the Father. His whole message was for us to love each other equally and how to enter Heaven by doing the will of the Father. He spoke the truth about how to become a spiritual being that we are all meant to be. And you Christians that say to people that do not believe in Jesus that they will perish. I tell you that you pass judgment when only God will judge. Jesus said if you judge you will be judged in like manner? He also said those who do the will of the Father are my brothers and sisters. Therefore before you take the splinter out of your brother's eye take the log out of yours. By judging you must make sure you are totally righteous with God, if not than you are in danger of damnation. Any act of judging belongs to God only.

You have heard the saying truth is truth, or the truth will set you free. Only the absolute truth can set you free. God is absolute truth.
Although this is a fictional story, with fictional characters there are many truths spoken in this book. And I am telling the truth about God the Father, what His intentions for all of us are, what He expects from us, and how all of us can receive His Power and gifts to help others.

Remember only God is good. I tried the best I can to explain as God has shown me. It may seem that I may be a little blunt in my explanations, but I didn't want to be too easy when I criticize all religions and people on earth for the way they have strayed away from God. The way people are acting toward each other. The way religions have fallen off the path of God not teaching, following and explaining in depth the Ten Commandments, and how we must cleanse our soul to enter Heaven. This book was written for all people on earth to be enlightened; it is for those who want to be on a spiritual path toward God the Father by His point of view not man's point of view. Although you may find it hard, if ye seek then ye shall find.

Armand J. Horta

I would like to thank God, who gave me the wisdom, knowledge, and the heart of flesh to understand Him and his feelings. And even though I am a sinner, and not totally righteous in His eyes, that He would chose me to bring you this message. I thank God for Jesus, because Jesus died showing us the truth and showed us how much love we are all suppose to have for each other. And I thank God for blessing me with His Holy Spirit, all the gifts I have received; the miracles I have seen, heard of by family and friends and been part of. And Father I thank you for how many times you saved my life from the grip of death.

I would like to thank Jessica Messotti for the typing of this book.

I would like to thank, Copycats of West Warwick, Rhode Island for the computer help and the excellent work they did in putting together the technical work for the cover and back page according to my design.

I would like to thank my wife Joan O. (Bouthillier) for editing and giving me helpful hints on how to make my writing be smoother, descriptive and correcting my English. And she was the photographer for the picture on the back cover.

I would also like to thank my wife, Joan, my three children, Jennifer, Jasmine, and Jacob, and my parents, Therese P. (Laframboise) Horta and Frank S. Horta Jr., for the love we have always shared together.

As you read this story, have an open mind and an open heart, and pray to God to show you the meaning of these words. If you do not grasp the full meaning, understanding and potential of being a child of God, read the four gospels and words of Christ until you do understand. Then reread this book. God is your Father, He will show you.

When you do understand, you will be shocked to think we live our lives in such an ignorant way, and put importance on things that are insignificant, when we could be so much more.

To prove evolution wrong, just open your mind to all the evidence available and think. Study especially the latest evidence in biology and the intricate study of genes and DNA. If you are searching for the meaning of life and believe in evolution you are searching in vain. Because in evolution life has no meaning, but a trillion to one chance that you could possibly exist as an intelligent life form. To prove God exist, it takes knowledge and faith. To prove Divine Intervention: all you have to do is open your mind, heart, ears, an eyes and look how intricate and complex the world is. You will have to agree, this all couldn't come about by chance. Also listen to those that have seen miracles or how God has intervened in their lives. God's work is still going on today. All you have to do is ask Him to open your eyes and you will see His work all around you.

In Loving Memory Of

Therese P. and Frank Silva Horta Jr.

TABLE OF CONTENTS

CHAPTER I

AJH MEETS SHELA AND JOHN

It was a clear summer morning; the sky was a beautiful shade of blue, with a few clouds here and there. The sun was rising, changing the lower clouds to a lovely shade of orange, and then yellow. With dew on the ground and the still morning air, you could smell the pine needles. The sun was shining through the dense woods on a man, about five feet nine inches tall, thin build, and dark complexion. He had long, dark brown curly hair, with a little gray near the temples and gray hairs here and there on his head. He also had a moustache and goatee with some gray hairs, no sideburns or facial hair on the sides. He had smiling eyes; they are a hazel-brown color that turned a shade of brownish green on certain days. He was wearing a white robe with a rope around his waist for a belt, a big wooden cross held on with woven boot lace around his neck, and sandals on his feet.

He looked like a guru as he walked through the woods. His name is Ajh, (pronounced Ajha). He was a man of God; even the animals could sense something different about him, as they followed him to the foot of the hill. Ajh turned to the animals and said, "I am sorry my friends, you will have to go" as he pet them on the head, "I have a job to do and you cannot come along."

He turned and started up the hill. He grabbed vines, poison ivy, shrubs, and roots, whatever he could get his hands on to pull himself up the steep hill. His sandals were slipping on the grass and weeds and his white robe kept getting in the way. The rope around his waist didn't help matters any, it kept getting caught on the vines and weeds. Then he stepped on his robe and fell. He sat down, threw his hands in the air, and shook his head. He sat for a few seconds to catch his breath, and then he smiled and started up the hill again.

As Ajh reached the top of the hill, he heard a lot of laughter. Making his way through the small shrubs and trees he stopped, and could see a group of motorcyclists. They were standing in a small clearing of sand and their motorcycles were off to the side on a gravel area with stones to hold up their bikes. There was an opening to the right that was also a dirt road leading into a large sandpit. To the right of Ajh were some bushes then the large sand pit, to his left the tree line started going up the hill and around the clearing where they were standing, the hill was covered with tall pine trees.

The motorcycle group was drunk and pushing themselves around. They were getting very rowdy. As Ajh looked around, his eyes became fixed on a young couple in the group; their names are Shela and John. They were laughing but it didn't appear like they had been drinking.

He gripped the cross around his neck, bowed his head down, closed his eyes, and said, "Father, give me strength." Making his way through the bushes, he tucked the cross inside his robe. He knew what was about to happen.

As Ajh walked into the opening, one of the girls spotted him and said "Hey, who's that?" They all turned around and looked at Ajh. The leader said, "Well, well, what have we got here, a guru?" They all laughed. Ajh answered, "No, I am Ajh." Someone in the gang said, "What's that, a disease?" They all started laughing again. "And what do you do" the leader asked as he bowed before him? Ajh answered, "I bring peace and I can bring God back into your life through the words of the scriptures." One of the girls said, "Oh no, he is a holy roller!" Some fell down laughing because they were so drunk.

The leader looked at Ajh and said, "Then you must believe in turning the other cheek?" Ajh replied, "Yes I do." The leader laughed, "Then turn man turn," as he hit Ajh across the face. Several others pushed Ajh back and forth while some of them would continue to hit him.

The two Ajh spotted out of the group, were trying to stop them. Ajh was pushed toward Shela and John. They stared at his face. His eye was swollen, his cheeks were bruised, and his nose and lips were bleeding. Just then, the leader turned Ajh around and hit hard across the jaw. The others were laughing as Ajh fell to the ground. John grabbed the leader's arm and said, "Come on man, enough is enough!" The leader, much bigger than John, hit him in the chest with both hands and knocked him down; "If you can't hack it man, get out!"

Shela yelled, "He's not moving!" John still on the ground in the sand crawled over to Ajh and turned him over. By the position of his jaw, it looked broken. John put his head over Ajh's heart and said, "I think he's dead."

Everyone scrambled for their bikes and took off. The leader staggered over to his bike, started it up, and said, "Well, he was looking for trouble, giving us all that Holy Roller bull," and then he took off.

By this time John got on his bike, started it up, and yelled out to Shela, "come on, let's get out of here!" Shela was standing, shaking, and staring at Ajh. She turned and ran to John, "What are we going to do!?" John said, "We are getting out of here, so get on!" Shela jumped on the bike; John gunned it and took off. The bike was kicking up dust going down the dirt road. You could see a cloud of dust in front of them from the other bikers. But the wind was blowing in the same direction they were heading; you had to keep moving so you wouldn't be covered in dust.

With the wind in their face and the noise of the bike they were yelling to talk to each other. Shela said, "Are you sure he was dead!?" John answered, "No, I don't know, I just said that so they would leave him alone! I couldn't feel or hear a heart beat, I'm not sure!" Shela said, "Then we have to go back and find out!" John answered, "If he is dead and we get caught near him, we will be blamed for his death!" Shela, getting nervous, "but if he is alive and we don't help him, we will be just as bad as they are!" As she pointed to the other bikers ahead.

John shook his head, "it's too risky!" Shela yelled, "Well if you're scared, then stop the bike and let me off, I'll go back alone!" John slowed down, and then he came to a stop, a cloud of dust covered them and they closed their eyes, then John looked at her. She grabbed his arm, "Please!" He shook his head, turned the bike around and headed back toward Ajh.

When they arrived back at the spot, Shela jumped off the bike and ran to where Ajh was lying in the sand, "he's gone!" John took a flat rock to put under the kickstand to hold his bike up. He ran over to look around. Shela's voice was in a panic, "Where can he be, where could he have gone!?" John said, "calm down, he has to be somewhere near by. These tracks, it looks like he dragged himself towards those trees."

They walked toward the edge of the woods, and started up the hill when they spotted him. They stopped suddenly and stared with amazement. There was Ajh sitting in a lotus position, in deep meditation. He was glowing with a white light, as a bright aura. (Very few people can see auras, but Shela and John were allowed to see it for their purpose.) Then the bruises on Ajh's face began to heal. His jaw straightened out, the swelling around his eyes disappeared, his nose stopped bleeding, and the blood disappeared. His whole face was healed. As the aura faded away, Ajh dropped back on the ground, he took a deep breath and sighed, and as if relieved of the ordeal he had just gone through.

Shela and John walked over slowly staring at Ajh, with their eyes wide open in disbelief. "A-ar-are you alright?" Shela asked stuttering. Ajh replied, "Yeah, I'm okay. I have to sit for a while." John looking bewildered, "how did you do that?" Ajh answered, "Very slowly." John asked, "How did you fix your jaw and your bruises?" Ajh replied, "Well actually, God did all of it, his energy healed me, you just have to learn how to control it."

Shela and John looked at him bewildered, "Are you serious?" Ajh answered, "of course, have you not seen people being healed and they pass out?" John said, "But that's not for real." Ajh responded, "There are phony healers and preachers and they will receive their just reward, but healings and miracles do happen. God's work is still going on. The reason people pass out is because they are overwhelmed by God's power and do not know what to expect."

"I remember once, when I first started doing God's work, I was in the woods, I fell off some rocks, and I had broken my leg. I asked God to heal me and I was overwhelmed by his power and passed out. A few hours later I woke up in the dark. I looked around and found myself in the middle of a pack of wolves. They were all staring at me. I was startled at first, but then I remembered I was with God. So I took a deep breath, relaxed, and called them over to me. They started licking my face. The leader even urinated on me. I guess he wanted to mark me as his territory!"
Shela was in disbelief, "How?" Ajh answered as he demonstrated, "well he just lifted his leg and squirted me, like this." "No, no" Shela said as she started laughing, "how did you tame them?"

Ajh smile, "it is easy when you become one with God." John asked, "How do you become one with God?" Ajh answered, "Just commit yourself to him and follow his laws. As Jesus said, *"Do the will of the Father."* Of course, prayer and fasting are important also."

"People do not realize how important it is to follow God's laws and to stay close to him. God gave Moses the Ten Commandments and no one seems to understand how deep the meaning is for each commandment. So people do not follow them as they should or realize how strict they should obey them. God sent Jesus and they crucified him. The Christians and the Jews follow the bible, yet they do not do the will of the Father the way He wants us too. Look how many Christian churches there are that have people of hate groups and factions that get involved in war, and they do not speak out against them. Many people practice some of their religion, but then the way of the world gets in the way. It becomes a wall between them and God, so they stray off the path of righteousness."

"Gandhi showed a nonviolent way to achieve peace and today his people are killing each other. The Muslims talk of holiness and a brotherhood of men doing God's will, yet they declare holy wars against each other and their neighbors. And do not treat woman with respect. What happened to *"Love thy neighbor as thyself"* and *"Thou shall not kill"* and only God is holy. The Chinese talk of wisdom, but there is no wisdom in denying people their freedom."

"In the East, certain religious groups or Yogis, meditate for months to gain certain powers, depending on what they are looking for. When they receive them, they show off in the public to amaze people. Never once do they give God credit for what they have. Nor are they thinking of God's way, for God does not show off or boast of his powers. He does not have to prove anything to anyone. To show off means to have pride, that is not God's way. And you should only use God's power to help others."

Ajh stood up and started climbing the hill, and they followed. "And preachers, who are given the gift to heal or utterance to preach the word of God, make themselves rich and powerful. They will not receive a welcoming entrance into Heaven." Jesus spoke of them; those who receive God's gifts and do nothing with it and those who use the gifts to make themselves rich and famous. They are not doing the will of the Father. Blessed are those who use their gifts in God's ways and seek nothing in return."

"Everyone has gifts from God; we must realize what they are and use them for God's purpose. Those who do nothing with the gifts are worthless and will be cast into hell. Those who use the gifts for fame and fortune are those who think they will enter into Heaven, but they are a thief and a robber. But those who use the gifts to help others and seek nothing in return will have a place in Heaven near God. So find out what your gifts are and use them not for your own purpose, but to help others. Feel God's presence in you, because God lives in us all."

John looked puzzled, "Then why does God give them the gifts at all when they will not use them in God's ways." Ajh sighed, "Well it is like this, if a child keeps asking his father for a car and continuously bothers him, the father will give the child a car hoping the child will learn the value of what was given to him. If a man will do this for his child, how much more will God, with endless love, give to you?"

Shela asked, "What about when people pray and their prayers are not answered?" Ajh shook his head, "so many do not understand God. The only ones that are not answered are the ones with very little faith. You see, when you pray, do not hope He will answer your prayers or pray repetitiously as if God does not hear you. But know in your heart that God heard you. If you believe, and have faith, without doubt, He will answer your prayers."

"Of course, there are instances where God does not answer prayers because he knows what is best. For example, if a person is dying and the family prays for a healing, but God knows that this person has become a sinner. If he or she lives they will become a worse sinner than they were before, and end up in hell. It is better to let that person's life end, then to spend eternity in hell."

"And there are those whose time is over and they must move on. I myself have seen it happen with my mother. My family and friends kept praying for a healing for her, she battled cancer for over 24 years. I know now it was our prayers that kept her alive. She would be healed then latter on it came back, we would pray and again be healed. I wondered when she died, why God did not answer my prayers again. Latter I realized it must have been time for her to move on, to go to heaven and be with God and that we kept her alive long enough. It is our own selfishness that keeps them alive, because we do not want to see them go even if they are suffering. God knows what is best. As for people that die before their time, it is the life we choose with out God, and the pollution we live in that causes an early death. I will explain in more detail latter."

"I know there are religions that teach God has power over life and death, which He does. But that does not mean God takes your life when He chooses too. God does not take a life, but allows life to take its natural course. Or how ever you live your life and what happens is your choice. He can extend it, but very seldom, if ever, takes a life because God is the River of Life."

As they were climbing the hill they could feel the warm sun on their backs coming through the trees. They were beginning to sweat even though there was a cool breeze coming across the hill. Ajh continued "but how many pray for help, yet their deeds and hearts are far from God. Many, the only time they pray, is when they are in trouble."

"Some people think of themselves as being religious and pray to God, yet they believe in astrology, crystal balls, card reading, curses, superstitions, and other false gods. You must believe in God only. Christ said, Ask and you shall receive, knock and the door will be opened. If you open your mind and heart to God, you will receive all kinds of knowledge, knowledge your modern science knows nothing about, let alone try to understand. You will realize these false beliefs can not affect you at all. You will see the true path toward God that Jesus spoke of."

All this time while Ajh was talking, they were climbing the hill a good distance. Then John realized how far they were from his bike. "Hey, my bike, someone might take my bike!" Ajh said, "Let who ever wants it keep it." John getting excited, "Are you crazy, that bike cost me over $8,000, and I did most of the work!" Ajh smiled, "How much will you lose without God in your life? After all, what is more valuable, the words of God or the ways of men?"

John hesitated, he did not know how to answer, he began to stutter, "I, I'm, I'm not giving up my bike to follow someone through the woods and probably getting lost!" Ajh replied, "Possess nothing of this world," Ajh paused, "go ahead, get on your bike and ride off. What will you gain? You will never know the real truth and it will haunt you the rest of your life. Can you walk out not knowing God's words or what true love from God is? Or what He has in store for you? Then you will be lost!"

John didn't know what to say, and getting nervous "let me hide the bike or sell it or something, Shela, why are we following him anyways?" Shela said, "I don't know, but I like what I hear, I feel something inside and it feels good. I'm going to stay." John said, "But you're my girl!" Ajh as he was walking up the hill, turned around, "I do not want your girl, I want my sister." Ajh continued up the hill.

Shela ran up to Ajh and grabbed his arm to stop him. "Wait!" She ran down to John, "John look, why don't we follow him for a while and if there is nothing more to his words, we'll come back for the bike." John thought for a second, "alright, we are pretty much out in the middle of nowhere, and I think I locked the front wheel."

They started up the hill, then John grabbed Shela's arm and turned his back towards Ajh. He put his hand in his pocket, pulled out a small bottle, opened it and poured out the contents into his left hand. It was ten tablets of acid. "Hey this guy is a real trip, why don't we make the trip worthwhile?" Shela shook her head, "no, he's going to be able to tell and I want to hear what he has to say." John looked at the tablets, separating them with his right index finger, and said, "come on, it will be as funny as hell."

Suddenly Ajh's hand appeared beside John's hand, with palm up, "I do not think it is funny and hell is nothing to laugh about! Put them in my hand!" John looked at Ajh with a disgusted look on his face as he put them in Ajh's hand. Ajh cupped his hand and put them all in his mouth at the same time. They were stunned as their eyes opened wide and their mouths dropped, Ajh turned and started up the hill.

John ran up in front of him, with an excited voice, "are you out of your mind, you are going to trip your butt off! You just took enough acid to drop an elephant! You could die!" Ajh looked at John as if annoyed and kept on walking, "it will have no effect on me whatsoever." Shela was stunned, "how is that possible!?" Ajh answered, "With God anything is possible."

Ajh stopped climbing, turned and looked at them, "because I do not want it to. Remember always these words of Jesus, "*There is nothing outside of man that can harm him, only that which comes from within can defile a man.*" So I believe without doubt that I will have no ill effect from the acid. All the positive thinking books in the world are based on that one sentence from Jesus, because it holds true to everything in life, even with disease, poisons, superstitions, and all kinds of false beliefs. Let us continue up the hill."

As they walked on the path climbing higher, the air felt cooler. Ajh continued, "according to Hindu beliefs, there is a saying, a person is the creator of his own fate. This is true, if a person does not follow the path of God, then whatever path they chose there will be danger, obstacles, and misfortunes. Some people think they can walk both paths and be safe. These are falsehoods brought on by thinking like the world. You are either of God or man. You choose your own fate"

"In Buddhism they say suffering is universal, this is not totally true. The suffering is caused by mankind, which I think is what they meant by universal. But Buddhism's second noble truth says, the cause of suffering is the craving or selfish desire. This is true and is the main reason for the problems of the world. Because we think of ourselves above others, we are selfish, greedy, vain, proud, and all the other sins that separate us from God, and because man believes in man, then we will suffer the consequences of the paths chosen."

"Come on, at the top of the hill there are some strawberry and blueberry bushes, we can rest there." Shela and John said, "Good" with relief in their voices, they were exhausted from climbing the hill. At the top there was a nice breeze, an in the shade of the pine trees it felt cool and relaxing. In the open area there were patches of blueberry and strawberry bushes, they picked some then sat down together.

While they were sitting down eating the wild berries, John asked, "Do you mean all the diseases we have are because of our beliefs in man and not?" Ajh interrupted, "well it is not just cut and dry like that, but basically yes. If man followed God and stood on the righteous path toward Him, things would be better in the world. If a person was close to God, that person would not be affected by disease or anything the world could throw at them, because they would have all the healing powers of God in them, and they would believe without doubt that God would take care of them. But to achieve this, you must totally be with God and want nothing of this world. Your heart and desires must be for Him and Him only."

"Christ gave many examples. He said, "*It is easier for a camel to go through the eye of a needle, than it is for a rich man to enter into the Kingdom of Heaven,* because if your heart and desires are here in this world, then how can you leave it to enter into Heaven where no materialistic things exist."

Shela asked, "But what about rich people that do a lot of good with their money?" Ajh answered, "It is not good enough, they still live in luxury while their brothers and sisters of the world are starving, homeless, and need medical treatment. Most people become rich by overcharging for their services. This shows they are not thinking of other people, because the average person has to dig deeper into their pockets. Normally most companies operate with cheap labor. So to be rich means to keep the poor "poor.""

"If a person is rich, they should ask themselves, how much money do I need to be happy? If they find God they would make sure all their employees are taken care of, and set up programs that would make employee life better. I am telling you that not all rich are going to hell, but they who make it will not reach a high place in Heaven. Most if not all rich are proud of their achievements, you must be humble and serve others to do God's work."

"If you were rich and you really found God in your heart, you would feel real good inside, and you would realize that the material things in this world, mean nothing. Then you would be giving your money away and it would feel good and you would want to give away more money to help more people and the feeling in your heart will grow, because

God is blessing you with the Holy Spirit. And when you give everything away and possess nothing of this world, you will see God."

There was a little silence; you could hear the birds chirping, the wind blowing through the pine needles and the branches swaying. The squirrels were chasing each other around the trees and the chipmunks were sending signals to each other that we were there. As the sun rose higher it was getting warmer.

John asked, "How about all these evangelists and religious leaders that have a lot of money? Sure they do a lot of good, but they themselves are rich in their three piece suits, nice homes, and nice cars." Ajh raised his hand with his index finger pointing and said, "Ah, why do you think Christ said, "*There will be many who do miracles in my name, and cast out demons in my name. But I will say to them on Judgment day, you do not know me, depart from me you who practice lawlessness.*" They are not doing the will of the Father, or what Jesus told them to do, to honor the Father and to live without possessions of material objects. Many of them honor Jesus more than the Father, and they are enjoying the wealth while spreading the word of God."

"There are those who are blessed and receive riches for doing God's work. God has rewarded them. But they must stay focus on doing God's will and do not posses material objects, and do not take large sums of money for pay. If you are truly of God you would not need all that money, because it will lead you away from God's true path. They must set an example being humble and without pride, thinking spiritually for this is the way to Godliness."

"It is pride, that which leads to material things, on a path away from God. Possessions are man's way of thinking that he needs all these things to live happily and to fulfill his life. If you live a spiritual life you do not need anything of this world. That was Christ's whole purpose in life, to bring people back to God as a spiritual being with the truth. If everyone understood what He was saying their eyes would be opened, because His Truth is the light of the world, and His truth will set your spirit Free."

CHAPTER II

EXPLAINING ABOUT GOD

Shela asked, "What is the Holy Spirit?" John said, "Yeah only Christians believe in three persons in one God. Are there three persons in one God?" Ajh replied, "Well yes, this is not easy to explain if you do not understand God. Actually, there are other religions that believe in three or many false gods in one God. Some religions think that each face or each personality of God is a different god that is part of the one true God. The Hindu's believe that there is One Supreme God that all other gods are from. But there is only one God. The Holy Spirit and Jesus are part of God the Father. You are part of God. God himself in Psalms said *"Ye are all Gods, sons of the Most High, but never the less, ye shall die like men because of your transgressions toward each other."*

"You see, you are part of Him. He lives in you, but if you stray away from Him and continually sin, then you lose your heritage. We do not realize how much we lose. And yes, He is always there for you, all you have to do is ask for forgiveness and you are forgiven. If you believe without doubt and have complete faith anything you ask will be given to you."

"As for God, there are only three persons. Let's explain it this way; you, yourself are a three fold nature person. We will use the words three fold nature instead of three persons; it puts things in a better perspective. For example, you have a body which is the material side, you have a soul which is the spiritual side, and you have a personality, which is the essence of you, something you give off. Some people that are sensitive can tell what kind of a person you are, just by looking at you. Or when you walk into a room people smile at you and feel joy because they can feel something different about you. They sense what kind of person you are."

"Now let's talk about God the Father first, let me explain who and what form or entity God is. He is pure thought, pure energy, pure light, and pure love. His love has no limits. He has good intentions for all of us. No matter how many times you reject Him, God still loves you. He is pure energy without material substance. He lives in a spiritual world, yet the physical world revolves around Him. God is the center of the universe. All the galaxies revolve around the center. Look at the universe as a giant bubble, continuously revolving around God. He is also the center of your heart and soul. God is the spark of life in us all. He is unlimited energy. Unlike energy the way we understand it. The energy we use gets burnt up or used, where as His energy is never ending. He is energy without material substance or a physical form. He is pure white light. He is pure thought; He only has the best of intentions for us."

Ajh paused for a few seconds and then continued. "Now we come to Christ, he is the body, the material form of God. You see, Jesus was not just born 2,000 years ago. He always was. In the bible in the beginning it says that the Word was with God, and God walked with man and on several occasions God appeared before man. This was Jesus, the body of God, because God the Father cannot exist in a body. He is too immense to exist in a small body; part of Him can, but not all of Him. He is too powerful to be contained in a physical form. When God did appear to man, it is written, "I had to cover my eyes, for His light was that of the sun." That is the light of His energy."

"When you hear of people that have died then come back to life, they say, "I saw this beautiful light at the end of the tunnel and I wanted to be with that light." That light is God. It is a blinding light to the eyes but very pleasing to the soul. Some people when they have died and come back to life, say they saw Jesus in the light. That is because Jesus came out of the light of God to speak to them. Jesus is spirit when He is with God the Father."

"God is not a body that sits on a throne and decides who lives and who dies, who is cripple and who walks, who has a poor life and who has a prosperous life. God is pure thought. He gave us the freedom to choose the kind of life we want."

Shela brought up a point, "But, a lot of people don't have a choice." Ajh replied, "But they do, they are following man and not God. You could walk away from it all but it would be hard. Your family and friends would say you are foolish and they would not understand. Because there are many pleasures in the materialistic world, you would have doubt if you are making the right decision. God's greatest gift to us is the freedom to choose. Now is the time to make the right choice."

John asked, "If he knew how we would turn out, why did he give us a choice?" Ajh answered "your parents expect you to live your life their way, yet you reject them and go your own way. If God would force the people to live by His rules, they would reject Him even more than they do today. How much more your Father in Heaven loves you. To let you be free, and grow even if you stumble and fall, then walk toward God, the joy in His heart is indescribable."

"But there are many who like the pit they live in because of all the pleasures the world has to offer, and do not want to hear the words of God. If you had felt the joy in God's heart when you two turned around to come after me, you would never sway off from God's path." Shela's eyes became watery.

John asked, "Then Jesus is the Son of God or is he God?" Ajh thought for a moment, "we are all his children but we are not pure like Jesus, and yes Jesus is His son. You see Christ was the body from the beginning of time, to walk on earth and communicate with man at his own level. That is why when Jesus was born, it was time to fulfill the scriptures, and a savior was needed. The truth had to be spoken. Jesus was born of God and a virgin woman. So he could live as a man and understand many ways and religions."

"He listened to many truths and as a child He read the scriptures, then he proclaimed God's truth. Jesus said, "I am the Son of God and I am the son of man. His truth was of one God, God the Father. He is part of God but not the whole. Just as your body is part of you but your spirit is what makes you whole. Jesus was born as a man to show you the way, a path and the words to be enlighten."

"Man made Jesus a God, even though He is part of God that is not what he wanted. When a man called Jesus *"good teacher"* Jesus stopped him and said, *"Why do you call me good, only God is good"* Jesus was trying to teach you to worship God the Father only and that through his words you will find the path toward God. Can you imagine Jesus saying He is not good, then what are we? How many of us hold our heads up high and think we are a good person. We are filled with so much pride, when we should be humble; it is the way to Godliness. Everything Jesus said came from God's mouth and was to teach you to do the will of the Father. This was man's destiny, an in return God would have taken care of us for all eternity. All the good Jesus did, he gave God all the credit for. We should do the same."

"When you pray, pray to God the Father. When you do all these things because of what Jesus taught you, and you do it in His name for God, you give Him honor. Do the will of the Father. That is all Jesus asks. Jesus said, *"I and the Father are one in the same you and I are one in the same."* "You see Jesus was trying to teach you, that if you follow Him you will be part of God too. He died so you can know the truth."

"By you being in God's way, then God lives in you. He can see the world through your eyes; feel the sand under your feet. He can smell the air; feel the wind all through your senses, if you let him into your life and your heart. He wants to live in you, let Him in. That is why we must live a righteous life and only see and do that which is righteous so that God lives in a pure temple of your heart. God needs you as much as you need him. For what is a Father, if he has no children."

Everyone was silent, just eating the berries under the trees. Shela asked, "And what about the Holy Spirit." Ajh answered, "oh yeah, I do take a while to explain things." They nodded their heads and John said with a mouth full of berries, "I never studied so much about God before." Ajh answered with a smile, "Just open your heart and you will do fine. I want to explain as much as I can so you can understand the truth. I can go into more detail if that would help." They shook their heads and laughed, "No, no, you're doing just fine."

Ajh smiled then continued; "Now the Holy Spirit, this is a little more difficult to understand. What I said before about a person's personality, how you can sense what kind of a person they are just by looking at them. Some times you can feel the goodness in them. It is something they give off."

"Well, the Holy Spirit is the essence of God, the part of Him that is given off from God. That is why He is called "Holy Spirit." God is a spirit and only God is holy. He is an individual like Jesus that blesses people with gifts that they need to do God's work, or they are blessed with a healing, or any of the many gifts from God. The Holy Spirit is part of God because God is pure energy, and only God can do this. To create a being that is part of Him, yet separate, to do a task to bring about the will of the Father."

"Like in the Old Testament, Moses, Solomon, and all the prophets, the miracles they did it was said they received the grace of God. They received the Holy Spirit. He comes in many forms, wisdom, knowledge, visions, joy the list is endless. They are all guidance toward a true path to do God's will. God has given the Holy Spirit of wisdom to all religious leaders, so there will be a true path toward God. It was given to Buddha, Confucius, Mohammed, Brahman, Jesus and all the prophets, and all the leaders of religions around the world. They are given the Holy Spirit of wisdom to guide people toward enlightenment even if they do not believe in God. Because He knows that all people need guidance or evil will truly overcome the Earth."

John wondered, "But all these religions say different things in their teachings, how can they all receive their wisdom from the same source and they don't believe in the same God?"

Ajh replied, "Remember the wisdom is coming from God but it is written down by man. Man is still influenced by the way he was brought up and the way he thinks. You also have to understand how often these scriptures have been translated and written down in different languages. And did the people who did the first or any of the translations have a true understanding. Also the words are changed to current beliefs and their own interpretation and teachings. That is why Jesus said, "Anyone that changes a word in the scriptures will perish in hell." So you see by changing the words you can derive different meanings and loose the truth of what is said."

"But the basics of all teachings for spiritual guidance follow the Ten Commandments. Any part of a religion that does not follow the Ten Commandments are words and thoughts of man. And John most of the religions believe in the same God they just give Him a different name and have different beliefs about Him. Look how many different Christian religions there are, and that goes for all the other religions as well. They all have different denominations. Believing what they want to believe."

Remember, the laws of God will put you on a path of truth, righteousness, and spiritual rewarding. Follow the laws of man and there is confusion, lies, and injustice, a path of ups and downs with restrictions. God gave ten simple rules to follow and if you follow them your life will be complete."

"Jesus has all the gifts from the Holy Spirit of God. That is why Jesus said "*I do nothing on my own, everything I say and do comes from God the Father.*" If you give God the credit for all the good things you do, the Holy Spirit of God will grow inside your heart. You will want to do more, and God's Spirit will flow through you to others, you will do miracles and many things in God's name."

John questioned, "You mean all those people, the Holy Rollers, have the power of God?" Ajh shaking his head and laughed, "No, they have received the joy of love from God." Shela asked, "Is that why Holy Rollers are always smiling and saying praise the lord, Hallelujah, and all that stuff?" Ajh laughed, "When you receive God's Holy Spirit you will jump for joy also, and prayer and fasting will help you become closer to God and the Holy Spirit will bless you with more. But you must seek more, remember always, *"Seek and you shall find, knock and the door will be opened."*

These people that receive the joy of God's love do not realize how close they are to doing miracles. All it takes is a leap of faith and what ever they ask will be done. They live every day filled with the joy in their hearts of God's love. All they have to do is take it a step further with faith and believe without doubt and they can do miracles. The answers for all that they seek are within their grasp. All they have to do is ask God and they shall receive. If they really understood the words of Jesus they would be doing miracles. God is always blessing people with the Holy Spirit and granting gifts. Jesus and the Holy Spirit are part of God the Father, but not all of Him. Jesus told you to worship the Father, and do His will. He spoke the truth we must listen to Him, it is very important to understand what Jesus was teaching us."

"I heard a preacher say that we are not born with love that we grow and understand what love is through Christ. If we are given a soul in the womb from God, who is pure love, and He gave us this soul out of love, then how can we be born without love? The fact is we are born with love and continually seek love as we grow. With the words and actions of Christ we understand what true love from God is, and how we are suppose to spread love to others. If we were born without love we would be Satan's children, seeking only selfish desires and thinking only of one' self. Some people loose their path from God and follow the path of evil because they enjoy the material things of the world instead of the spiritual things from God and they have no love in them."

Ajh looked off to the side and he saw a small bush. He went over to get a better look. Ajh, with excitement in his voice, "Oh great, I have not tasted these in a long time!" They both walked over to where Ajh was crouched down in front of a small bush stuffing his mouth with little red berries. John asked, "What are these" as both of them put some berries in their mouths? Ajh answered, "I do not know, they have a very strong tart taste to them."

They were eating quite a lot of them, squinting their faces and puckering their lips going "MMM." Then Ajh said, "I would not eat too many of them if I were you." John with a mouthful wondered, "Why not, they're good?" Ajh looked up at them as he was still crouched down by the bush, "because they are poisonous."

Shela and John began choking and spitting out what they could. John getting excited, "Are you crazy!? Sheila asked still choking, "Why are you eating them!?" Then Ajh stood up, "you are not listening to me are you? *"There is nothing outside of man that can harm him, only that which comes from within."* I believe in the words of Jesus."

Ajh walked around the bush and kept walking away, there was a smirk across his face. John picked up a dead pine branch, like he wanted to hit Ajh with it, but he turned to hit a tree, like he was mad and frustrated. Shela ran up to Ajh, "Are we going to get sick?" Ajh smiled, "no, you did not eat enough. Besides just believe in those words without doubt and you will be alright." Shela stopped walking; looking at John they started shaking their heads.

Ajh continued walking ahead of them. She ran up ahead to catch up with him and asked, "How come you believe in God and Jesus, yet you don't say praise the lord and alleluia like the others do?"

Ajh stopped walking and looked at her, "for two reasons, one I do not have to show mankind how I feel about God. I keep the feeling inside me, so only God knows. The second reason is most reborn Christians are turning people off by their way of expressing themselves. I mean it is ok with people of the same faith, and people that feel the same way. But people that are not religious, it turns them off. You cannot have a conversation with them without them trying to convert you or get you to join their church. This turns people away from church and God. That is the last thing I want to do, especially with those who are not of God."

"So I keep God inside my heart; then people can sense how happy I am; there is something about me, the things I do and the way I am dressed that makes them curious. Shela said, "It made me curious."
Ajh continued, "They want to know what I know. And because they ask, their ears will be open to hear. Maybe someone will be saved instead of being turned off. If I was saying praise the Lord and alleluia would you two still be following me?"

"Let your heart be a temple for God, so His Holy Spirit flows through you and He will let you know what to say. When you are talking to someone that is not of God, weave into the conversation that you thank God for all the good things He has done for you. Let them go home not feeling like they are smothered with religion, but asking themselves what am I doing wrong, what am I missing out of, can God help me too?"

"If you let the Holy Spirit fill you, you will know how to approach people differently. The Holy Spirit will speak through you and you will capture the person's mind and heart. Let God do the talking."

"If you dress more conservative they will ask why. You might influence them instead of them influencing you. Remember God knows what is in your heart and that is all that matters. Do good so only God knows and tell man nothing, or the good you have done will mean nothing by your boasting and your pride. Man's ego is what separates him from God. Humble yourself, possess nothing, and give God the credit for all the good that you do. This is how to be a child of God."

"As they say in the Eastern religions, take your ego and shatter it on a rock. It is your ego that makes you think you are better than everyone else. We are all equal in God's eyes. There for everyone you see is your brother and sister. We are here to serve and help each other and to do God's will. God's intentions for mankind were to live on Earth as gods, doing His will. He lives in us, we live in Him, and if we lived by His rules He would have taken care of us for all eternity."

"Do away with pride, because pride makes you think you are doing things on your own without God's help. Be humble, serving others for this is a way toward God. If you learn to be silent and listen you will receive wisdom. If you try to understand everything around you, you will gain knowledge. The gifts of God are many, you must seek them. He is very gracious."

Chapter III

Ajh begins explaining the Ten Commandments

They continued on into the woods, leaving the berry patch behind. Besides, after the poison berries, Shela and John were not feeling hungry anymore. Ajh was walking ahead of them and said, "now where was I, oh, it does not matter, how about I explain the Ten Commandments. They both looked at each other and shook their heads. Ajh still looking forward, "do not shake your heads, just listen." They looked at each other wondering how he knew what they were doing.

Ajh continued, "Before I start, look at the Ten Commandments in two ways. First, as a way toward God and a spiritual guidance of enlightenment, second, look at the commandments as a way of a higher intelligence. Even if you were an intelligent atheist, you would have to agree following the Ten Commandments would make a better society. A society that would prosper and grow, instead of a society that is deteriorating and becoming stagnant as the world is doing today. We may be advancing in technology, but our morals and respect for each other are declining. This will eventually affect our technology."

"As a society deteriorates it is easier for Satan to move in because he is of ignorance and demoralizing. Satan teaches people to look out for number one, and seek vengeance against someone that oppresses you and do things that are immoral. As a society becomes more and more immoral soon even technology will slow down. Because there will be less people to carry on the more intelligent work needed to advance."

Ajh paused as they were walking, "now the first commandment, *I am the Lord thy God and thou shalt not have false Gods before me and thou shalt not make unto thee any graven image of Heaven and earth, nor bow down to them, nor serve them.*"

"This is self-explanatory, but people do not realize how much love they are supposed to give God. People give objects more love and attention then they give the Father. They idealize a musician or movie star more than The Almighty. If they felt that way about God, they would receive a lot more in return. It would not cost anything except time and how much time does it take to tell God you love Him?"

"A lot of people believe in lucky rabbit's foot, lucky coins, astrology, crystals, tarot cards, etc. These are all false gods, because you believe in something other than God having an affect on your life. Everyone must believe in God only, because everything else is nonsense and superstition."

John asked, "And what about when these false beliefs have an affect on people's lives?" Ajh answered, "There is no effect at all, and actually it is the mind. People do not realize how powerful the mind is. Take astrology for example. The mind helps influence others to make your beliefs to come true. Your mind knows what you read in your sign, so you follow through with it to make it come true, whether it is bad or good because this is what you believe in. All these things, card reading, crystal balls, astrology, or anything else people believe in are false gods, because they are not of God. Satan has influenced the world to believe in false gods, and he helps these things come about to deceive you."

"Some of these beliefs are imprinted from childhood. Look at the cartoons with magical crystals, magic cards and so on. When you grow up you realize it is fictional, yet you start believing in healing crystals and stones, curses and what ever else is not of God. Even if you believe in curses, it is against God, because you do not have enough faith in God that He will protect you. Remember, nothing on the outside of man can harm him, only that which comes from within. If you are of God then you would not believe in curses, and you know they can not affect you."

How often people only know or talk to God when they are in trouble, or say they believe in God when it is convenient. How can you say you love someone when you only say it once in a while?"

Ajh paused, "God does not listen to cold hearts when he knows they will stay cold, but someone who begs for forgiveness and God knows their heart is open and will try to mend their ways, He listens. No matter how terrible, how immoral, or how sinful this person has been, or how many times this person has failed, God will stretch out his hands to forgive, help, and guide this person by sending others that can show them the way to salvation."

"Remember always, God is your Father. Tell Him every day that you love Him and talk to Him everyday. He listens and will answer. Maybe not in a way you expect, but He will answer. All you have to do is ask and you shall receive."

"There will be many ways in which God will answer and guide you. Many people seek guidance through false beliefs. But if you want guidance, or even to know your future, take a bible and open it. Wherever it opens to, read both pages, and if the chapter started a few lines before and after those pages read them too. Sometimes you can tell right away that what you are reading pertains to you."

"If you do not understand what it means, just think about what you read and put the book down. In a few days something will happen and remind you of the scriptures you read, you will have a better understanding and know a deeper meaning of the words in the bible. Seek God and ye shall find him, knock and the door will be opened, it is all there for us, we just have to ask with an open heart. Ask and knowledge can be yours."

"Before I was on the path of following God as I am today, I owned a small business, I was being robbed and vandalized a lot, but this one time I lost a lot of money. As I closed the store at the end of the day, it was still eating at me. As I drove my van down the street I was blind with rage. I was not paying attention to anything, not even my driving. Finally I snapped out of my rage long enough to look to the right side of the road at a statue of Jesus on the lawn with his arms stretched out. All my hatred disappeared, and I laughed. That was real good God, sneaky but good."

Ajh stopped walking, turned and looked at Shela and John. But they looked at him puzzled, "you do not understand? God snapped me out of my hatred to look at the statue. As if Jesus was reaching out saying, hey remember me and what I stand for. All my hatred was gone and I felt God and Jesus so close, inside my heart. Then I said Father forgive those kids for they know not what they do. I said a prayer for them and I felt real good inside. They should have statues of Christ everywhere."

Shela asked, "But aren't statues graven images, what you said was in the first commandment?" Ajh replied, "this is true, if everyone was totally with God, we would not need them, but sometimes you need a reminder, not something to pray to, but just a reminder to put you back on the right path. Maybe they should have the Ten Commandments in front of all the courthouses and government buildings." John remarked, "you can't have religious objects on public land remember, separation of church and state."

Ajh answered, "There is some truth to that, separation of church and state, yes, separation of God and state, never. This country was founded on the belief of God. And remember this, Jesus himself is not a religion, but a man that stood for absolute love and a way of life toward God.

Anyone that does not want a statue of Jesus on government property is against Christ."

John said, "But there were Christians who fought against the nativity scene on state land." Ajh replied, "Remember Jesus said, *"Those who call themselves Jews and are not,"* well the same goes for Christians. There are many who call themselves Christians, yet have no idea what Jesus was all about, what he stood for, or what he was trying to teach us. Jesus said, *"Either you are for me or you are against me."*

"There are people who have abortions and think it is their right and those who fight against the Nativity Scene or taking God out of the schools, are joining a small group of people that are part of an atheistic cult of Lucifer's underlings. Satan keeps them blind of what he is really doing. These people that fight against the nativity scene they do not argue when their boss gives them Christmas day off, or when wars stop or have a cease fire to honor Christ. They are hypocrites."

"The nativity scene is actually a symbol of the birth of a man who lived 2,000 years ago and to this day no one has ever shown as much love for mankind as Jesus did and no person has had an effect on the world as He has. So why not honor Him, like they do so many others that have made a mark in history."

"A true Christian would not stop symbols of true love from being displayed. Those that do are hypocrites, just like those that crucified Jesus. Like abortions, how many Christians either have abortions or fight for the right for others to have them. They are helping people commit a hideous crime against God. Life begins when one consumes."

"Some people say the child is not human yet. Well it is not a plant or animal. Some say it is not alive because it has not been born. While the child is in the womb, the child is breathing, eating, and growing. According to science, that means it is a living being. Even a plant does this and you call it a living thing. If you cut a plant from the roots you say you killed it. Why is it if they cut a child from its life source they call it an abortion does it make it any easier? And if it is alive and you stop, or snuff, or cut, or whatever word you use to abort that process, then you have killed the child." You could hear the anger in Ajh's voice as he continued.

"I know life is very hard today to raise a family, but abortion is not the answer. Even in the case of rape or incest, you are still killing the child. If you should find yourself in that situation then bear the child until you can give up the child for adoption. There are many couples that want children and can not have them. And do not think that the child will have the same characteristics as the father because that is a lot of bull. A child only imitates what they see, hear, and is taught. If a child knows only love then the child will only give love in return."

"If a woman finds herself in this situation she should seek counseling and support until she gives up the child for adoption. If Jesus was whipped beaten and crucified to show how much love we are supposed to have for each other. And nailed to the cross He asked God to forgive them. How small of a sacrifice is it to bear the child for nine months until you give it up for adoption."

"To those who still believe it is all right, the first time they had an abortion, they had to do some thinking, whether to have it done or not. That is because there was a spark in their subconscious that told them it was wrong. But the more excuses they thought of the more they convinced themselves it was all right. But they would have to ask themselves this, if God was standing in the room would they still go through with it."

"The argument is a woman has the right to do whatever she wants to her body, but in actuality, there is nothing being done to her body. Everything is being done to the child's body and if you do not tell people it is wrong, then the sin will be on your head when it comes to judgment day."

"This is written in the bible in the words of Jesus and Ezekiel, chapter 3, verse 18-21. If you tell them it is wrong and they do not listen to you, then you are cleansed of the sin, but if you say nothing because you are afraid of what they will think of you and do not warn them of God's punishment, the blood will be on your head."

"Some people call for capitol punishment, when God says *"thou shalt not kill."* When Cain slew Abel, God cast Cain off away from the others, and said no man must lift a hand against him. God was setting an example for you, judge not and ye shall not be judged."

Shela asked, "Then what do we do with all the criminals." Ajh answered, "Just cast them away from society where they cannot harm anyone. Put them on an island or some place desolate. Let them work for themselves. Even if you keep them in a prison make them work to pay their debt to society. And teach them the word of God to save their souls."

"There are a lot of ways you could deal with society's problems and still stay with God. But if you execute someone for their crimes against humanity, they do not have a chance to tell God they are sorry. If they are allowed to live out their lives, they have a chance to be saved and have a place in Heaven."

As they were walking, they were coming to a clearing on the hillside. It was very rocky and the path weaved in and out around large boulders. Ajh continued, "I know there are preachers out there who are for abortions and the death penalty and other things that are really against God. That is why you have to beware of false prophets in sheep's clothing, only some of them wear three piece suits of wool, polyester, and cotton."

"If a preacher gets on the wrong track and says things that are not of the Ten Commandments, then it is the people's responsibility to set him straight. If he refuses to listen, then walk away from him and the church he preaches at, because he will slowly lead you to a path away from God. A good preacher is always speaking of the truth and he is humble and selfless. What he says feels good in your heart and he is not rich in money or possessions. Then you know he is a man of God."

"It should be easy to tell false prophets when you see and hear them preach. They will disguise themselves with words of Christ and love. They know how to use the right words to draw your attention so you will listen to them. They will speak the words of God, but they are false prophets. They will shout these words to make themselves sound important, taking money and buying many possessions instead of spreading the truth and helping others. If they do not repeat the words of the scriptures and explain them, if they do not follow the path and words of Jesus and what He talked about, and they do not teach the meaning of the Ten Commandments, then walk away."

"And if they say they are Jesus, know in your heart they lie because Jesus told you when He comes he will come out of the clouds from the east and to the west, and all the people on earth will see him. In the end Satan will send many false prophets because he knows his time is up, he wants to take as many people as he can with him to hell."

Suddenly they heard some voices and all three of them turned around and saw an overweight sheriff and his tall thin deputy coming over the hill. The sheriff yelled, "Wait up!" They were finding it difficult to walk on the stones. As he came up to them he was out of breath and could hardly talk. "Who owns that bike" puffed the sheriff? Ajh spoke up before John could say anything. "What is wrong officer?" The sheriff said, "We just arrested a bunch of motorcycle freaks in town. One of them started babbling something like; we didn't mean to kill him and said they beat up some guru in a white robe out by the sand pits."

While the sheriff was talking, he was eying out Shela. She is a beautiful, young woman, about 5 ft. 7 inches tall, well shaped, dark golden blond hair, blue eyes, in tight and very short cut off jeans, braless in a cut T-shirt. John was a good looking young man, 5 ft. 9 inches tall, wearing cut off jeans, cut sweatshirt; he had dark hair, dark complexion, and brown eyes and was very rugged. The sheriff couldn't take his eyes off of Shela as he smiled. Ajh stepped between them to break his concentration; he knew what the sheriff was thinking about.

Ajh said, "I'm the only one around here with a white robe and as you can see I am fine." The sheriff looked at Ajh with a disgusted look, "and what is your name?" "Ajh, this is Shela and John. They have been with me." The sheriff said, "Whose bike is that?" Ajh answered quickly again, "not ours, I would look pretty silly on a motorcycle, do you think?"

The sheriff giving Ajh a disgusted look and keeping his eyes on Shela, "Well, why don't you come into town so we can check you out." Ajh said, "I am sorry officer, but we do not have time and we are heading this way and also you are not going to get Shela to participate in your little nest of runaway whores." John and Shela were surprised at Ajh's words.

The sheriff getting very angry and his face turned red, "you better keep your mouth shut mister, or I'll slap the book on you!" Ajh held a bible in front of his face, "you mean this one?" The sheriff was getting excited and angry and he started yelling, "You think your pretty smart don't you!" Deputy, arrest this man and them too!" The deputy asked, "On what charge sir?" The sheriff answered, "We'll find something when we get into town!" Ajh said, "you will not be arresting anyone sheriff." The sheriff yelled, "that's it deputy, resisting an arrest!"

Before the deputy could get out the handcuffs, Ajh raised his hand with a bible in it. The wind began to blow. "You better leave sheriff before God consumes your dark soul and sends you to the pits of hell!" When he finished saying this he raised his hand a little higher and the wind became stronger and the trees began to sway. Dust was blowing all around making it hard to see. They were all finding it difficult to stand up except Ajh.

Fear started to come over the deputy and sheriff. Suddenly a bolt of lightning came down and hit a large boulder just below them and split it in two. That was all they needed, the sheriff and deputy started running and screaming, "my God, let's get out of here!" Stumbling over the rocks they ran as fast as they could. A second bolt of lightning came down over the hill and there was a big explosion that erupted. Shela and John were hanging on to each other. There was a big cloud of dust that covered the hillside.

Then just as fast as the wind came, it disappeared. John said wiping the dust off his face, "What happened!?" Ajh sat down in a meditation position and said, "Wait and be still." They both looked at each other and shrugged their shoulders wondering, what is he doing now? As they continued brushing the dust off themselves. Ajh sat there in deep meditation for about a minute, then he opened his eyes and stood up.

Shela asked, "What did you do, and what did you mean, wanting me for his little nest of whores!?" John asked, "Yeah, what was that all about?" Ajh answered, "Well apparently the sheriff here seems to collect all the runaways and others in his territory with his false arrest and he puts them in a house outside of town. That is where all your friends are from the motorcycle gang."

John and Shela said, "We only traveled with those people since yesterday, we didn't know they were like that. We thought we take a break from college and travel around on my bike." Ajh continued, "Well that is where they ended up, men in work camps as rented workers and women in whorehouses and look at you Shela, the way you are dressed, like a sex object for one of his senator friends. He would have received a good price for you." "Like hell he would have" yelled Shela! Ajh replied, "Well he would have beaten you, or kept you locked up until you agreed."

John asked, "What do you mean, his senator friends, and how do you know all this?" Ajh answered, "I read his mind, it was all he was thinking about. He has these sex parties for senators, congressmen, and some big businessmen who all like young girls, some as young as 16. When I was meditating, I notified the district attorney what the sheriff was up to, so he will take the proper steps and notify the FBI and state police. And I also notified a young reporter who is not particularly fond of the sheriff."

John asked, "How do you contact people?" Ajh answered, "Well it is like telepathy, but without words, like leaving an impression on their minds so they will follow through. The DA is a young, honest man. He feels the sheriff is up to no good, but whenever he tries to do something about it, his superiors have been pulling strings and telling him to leave the sheriff alone. Between the DA, the reporter, the FBI, and the state police nothing will be squashed, they will all get prosecuted.

John said, "Boy these people are scum!" Ajh remarked, "Do not judge." John getting a little upset, "What do you mean, you are going to tell me you think!?" Ajh interrupted, "no, I'm only saying judge not and ye shall not be judged. I am sure there are things in your past you would not want to discuss." John tilted his head down and became quiet. Shela asked, "How do you know all this stuff about these people?" Ajh answered, as he looked at them with a questionable look on his face, "God, who else. If you do not believe me you ask Him." They looked at each other and shook their heads, like saying is he for real? But the things they saw Ajh do kept them curious so they continued following him.

Ajh started walking and they were right behind him. Then John said, "Hey man, you lied, we caught you in a lie!" Ajh turned to look at John. "What do you mean?" John smiling, "You told the sheriff that we have been with you all the time and that the bike was not ours!" Shela smiling and pointing at Ajh, "yeah that's right, now where's all that Holy Roller stuff,?" as they both started laughing.

Ajh smiling, "hold on a minute, all I said was you have been with me. I did not say how long. That is not lying. He interpreted what I said wrong, it is misleading but I think God would have approved." They both had a smirk look on their faces, "sure, sure." Ajh continued, "Well I did not want to use the power of God to convince them to leave, but I had no choice."

Then John remarked, "What about the bike, you said it wasn't ours, now get yourself out of that one?" Ajh smiling, "I know, I know, but actually it was not ours, it was yours. And you gave it up for all this great information I am giving you about God and how to save yourselves from the pits of hell." Ajh continued walking.

John thought for a second, "Wait a minute, I didn't give it up, and what do mean, it was my bike!?" Ajh turned around and looked at John with a grin on his face, "What do you think that explosion from the second bolt of lightning was?"

Ajh turned and walked away as he chuckled and tried to hold it in. John's face dropped, he was stunned. Shela was shocked and bit her lower lip as she tried to stop laughing out loud. John finally snapping out of it, started yelling, "Are you out of your mind, do you know how much that bike cost me!?" Ajh stopped walking, turned around and said, "$8,845.98 and you did most of the work."

By this time Shela was on the ground laughing. John looked at her, "Oh you think it's funny don't you, well I don't!" Ajh said, "consider it a small price to pay for what you are about to learn. Besides, store your treasures in Heaven where thieves cannot steal and your treasures cannot rot. Possess nothing of this earth, you will find it much more rewarding and satisfying."

John started yelling, "When, when I'm dead!? A lot of good that will do me then!" Ajh replied, "But that is when you will need it the most. It is because you do not know what lies ahead, beyond the physical life, is why you are saying that. If you knew what the Kingdom of Heaven is like, from this day forward you would spend every waking hour talking and praying to God and you would possess nothing of this world to make sure nothing stops you from entering into Heaven."

John was standing off to the side. He was really mad an upset about the loss of his bike. Shela asked, "I don't understand, what does possessing of a bike to get around with have to do with entering Heaven?" Ajh said, "I told you before, if you possess so many materialistic things, then how can you enter a spiritual world. Your desires, your wants are of a material value, they tie you down to a material world. Look how upset he is, over a material object." Shela said, "But he worked hard on that bike." Ajh answered, "I know it is hard for you to understand, but in three days if you seek God with your heart you will understand. This is why the rich very seldom enter into Heaven. They have many possessions and live for the enjoyment of these possessions, just like the poor."

Shela looked puzzled, "What; the poor, what do they have?" Ajh answered, "They have many possessions in their hearts, and they desire what the rich have. Their goal in life is to become rich, yet they curse the rich for having so much while they have so little. Their hearts and desires are of this world instead of being with God. One of the commandments says "*Thou shalt not covet your neighbor's wife, house, or anything belonging to someone else,*" covet means to want, desire, or crave."

"Enough about possessions, I told you before, you have to listen, we do not have much time." Ajh paused, "now let's see, where was I, I covered the first commandment, false gods, idols, graven images." Shela asked, "People don't really worship idols, or graven images do they?" Ajh answered, "Idols are still being worshiped around the world today. There are a lot of false gods. Look at movie and TV stars, people idealize these stars a lot. People spend much of their time and money buying their products and reading all about their idols, watching them on TV. If they spent that much time idealizing and reading about God, they would be perfect, spending their money on good causes, they would find it much more rewarding; their life would be filled with joy."

"How many people have statues or painting or other objects they adore and love more then they say they love God." There are religions that bless statues, kneel and pray before them, this is a sin against God because there is nothing or anyone in the statue, these are all graven images and you do not have to travel to pray to God. All you have to do is close your eyes and pray. For God is always in your heart and He always hears you. And do not pray to saints, monks, high priest or whoever, only to God."

And how often if a child breaks an object of value, the adult will scold and punish the child, putting their feelings of a material object over the feelings of a child. "*Suffer the children not, for theirs is the Kingdom of Heaven.*" I know we must teach our children discipline, but the feelings of a child are more important than an object. Parenting takes patients and wisdom."

"Among the Muslim truths they have a saying, yet in mankind are some who take unto themselves objects of worship, which they set as rivals to Allah, loving them with a love that which belongs to Allah alone. Allah is the name they have given God."

"To show you how simple and down to earth God is, He said to build an altar for offerings, to make it out of fieldstone and earth and let no tools carve into it. Another words, nothing fancy just stone and dirt. God likes things plain and simple. Look how religions of the world, even some Christian religions make their altars with carved stone, gold and jewels embedded into it. Most religions do not listen to God and do what He wants."

They continued walking, it was a beautiful day, and the sun was warm. They were still walking on the rocky path and in a little distance it was sandy with some weeds growing in a clearing, with only a few small trees in the opening. Off in the distance the tree line started again. In the open area you could see more of the landscape with the hills and a grassy area ahead.

Shela asked "Where are you from, you speak differently?" I am from God, and reading the Bible a lot I ended up using the same word phrases. I'm also from Rhode Island. People from other states make fun of the way we do not pronounce all the letters in a word. Like the letter R for example, we do not pronounce it as much as Massachusetts people do: we have kind of slang to a lot of our words or using the word got. We add the letter S to words that do not have an S like, yous an so on, people were always correcting me."

Ajh continued, "let's see, next we shall cover "*Thou shalt not take the name of the Lord in vain.*" Using God's name lightly or in vain, and God will not let him go unpunished. But let's take this a step further; you should not use any foul language. When you swear or use foul language, you do not sound intelligent. If you stubbed your toe and said Abraham Lincoln or George Washington it would sound silly, would it not? Well then, why when people use God's name, does it sound right to them? Only use God's name in prayer or calling on him to talk, remember His name is holy."

"Let's see, the commandment that is next is "*Thou shalt keep holy the Lord's Day, six days you shall labor, but on the Sabbath ye shall not work.*" This was intended to give man rest from worldly things and to think spiritually. There were no such thing as going to churches or temples back then. You were to rest; even your servants and animals were not supposed to work. The meals were prepared the day before. God rested on that day; you should also rest on that day."

"People can pick their own Sabbath if they have to work on that day, just keep it holy. Spend time with God in your heart. Forget the materialistic world. Instead, enjoy and spend time in the spiritual world. When you enjoy the world He created," as Ajh looked around and at the sky, "you will fill your heart and body with His Holy Spirit and with His Light."

"Let God enjoy the world through you. Take off your shoes. Let God feel the sand and grass under your feet. Let Him feel the wind on your face. Let Him see the beauty of the world through your eyes. Talk to Him as you talk to your friends and relatives. Once you let God inside you and you become close to Him, you will see life differently and will understand God and His purpose for you."

"If you do not talk to God and you go a lot of days without him in your life, soon there is no God in your life, only worldly possessions and without God you are a living corpse, the walking dead. Because God is the light of all that lives, He is the spark of life that you are born with and also that which makes you good. If you nourish, this goodness in you, it will grow until your whole body is filled with His Light."

"That is why Jesus said, "*When thy eye be single, thy whole body is filled with light.*" He was saying that if you look at things in a righteous way, a single eye and only see good and not evil, God will grow inside you until your whole body is filled with His Light."

"A lot of Yogis or Gurus practice what they call the third eye or enlightenment. They meditate for months on end to achieve this. But if you listen to Jesus and follow his footsteps you will find it much more rewarding and easier, because He will help you if your heart is turned over to God."

"Most religions speak of enlightenment, only because it is written in the scriptures, but very few know how to teach it. They do not explain enough in detail how to prepare your soul or what you should do to enter Heaven. Or what God expects of us and how we can receive His power. I will explain more about this latter."

"Now getting back to the Sabbath, this commandment does not mean you have to go to church." John asked, "Then why do religions preach, going to church is what God wants?" Ajh said, "Well for several reasons, one through centuries of tradition, misinterpreting the commandment, and some so they can collect donations every week, but mostly it helps people stay close to God, which is good if you are the type of person who needs continuous fellowship. When you are at church and everyone praying together you can feel the presence of God, Jesus and the Holy Spirit."

"Most churches you go too all they talk about is how they need more money, they call it tithe. They want you to give 10% because it is written in the Bible. But it is also written in Genesis that Jacob told God he would give Him 20%. If we gave the church even the 10% of our pay check it means we would not be able to give to any other charity. Especially today the cost of living is so high. I myself liked giving too different charities, to see my money helping people and causes I support. This is still giving to God."

"As for going to church, even if you do not need a continuous practice of going to church, your children will need it. Because they are being taught by the parents what is good an evil and about God, but not on a daily bases. The kids go to school and are hearing hundreds of other kids saying things against God every day. The teachers with their teachings and beliefs of evolution are misguiding the children which is saying, there is no God."

"By going to church, children can make friends and hear the word of God often. When they grow up lacking God's presence in their daily lives, by the time they are in their teens or early twenties they will have their own interpretation of what is good and evil and it has nothing to do with God. And each generation will grow farther away from God until you have an adulterous and immoral generation that you have today".

"I know sometimes you have dead preachers with a dead congregation. People go to church or temple every week and are bored. They go through the motions but their hearts are not into it. These people will eventually lose faith. People should find a church that preaches about God and what He wants of us, and that we are worthy of His gifts. Then the whole congregation is alive with the Holy Spirit."

"When you pray, think of your whole body being filled with His light and pray with the spirit. It is good to go to church or temple to form a spiritual growth with other people, especially if you need this to stay straight with God. You will find friends at church that will help you grow close to Him in a spiritual way."

"But in your daily life if your friends are not close to God and their language and ways stray you away from Him, and you can not change them to turn to God, then you must stay away from these people and find those who are close to God to keep your spirit strong. If your friends ask you, why you do not hangout with them anymore, be honest tell them it is because of their language or their jokes or what ever it is that is not of God. Say it in a nice way, so they will listen. Maybe they will understand, maybe they will not, but at least you told the truth and they might think about it. Maybe someone will think enough to see your point of view."

"You should always practice kindness, caring, and loving people, showing understanding even to your enemies, then you are building the kind of church that Christ talked about, that God will accept. Build a temple of God in your heart. That is where the true church belongs. This has been written in Revelations; the Church of Philadelphia is your heart. And remember Jesus said, "*The Sabbath was made for man, not man for the Sabbath."*

"In the Hindu beliefs, it says; "He whose mind is always fixed on God requires no other practice, devotion, or exercise. In the Muslim truths it is said; "God said whoever has true knowledge of the scriptures is sufficient witness between me and you." But this means true knowledge not your own particular interpretation, which a lot of people do today."

"Let God grow in your heart, let your mind be fixed on him always. If you spread love all around you and it keeps spreading around the world, you will see the problems of the world diminish to nothing. When you go to church find one that preaches of enlightenment and truth, then you can feel it in your heart." John said, "You don't find too many churches like that." Ajh answered, "no, but they are growing. It is time for enlightenment in the world."

"It is too bad there are many preachers who do not know the truth and just mimic the words in the bible, and there are preachers who are seeking money, and that turns people away from religion all together."

"Some religious organizations are so rich they could feed all the starving people in the world if they sold all their assets. Instead, they only feed the poor on the interest of what is left over. And there are some preachers who call for capitol punishment and praising our government for helping other countries in war, even though God said "*Thou shalt not kill*". They rewrite the bible as they see it, to accommodate modern beliefs and interpretations."

"Some preachers build bible colleges in their name, they nurture some people's minds while others are starving. Yet all the knowledge in the world is not equal to what God can bless you with. These preachers are being paid so much, when if they were with God, they would only need the essentials to be comfortable."

"People themselves should not become discouraged because they continually fall off God's path. If you follow God, and you look back at your life before, you will be able to see how far off the path from God you were. Then as you continue on your journey, and become closer to God, you will look back and see you still have swayed off the path. Some people would become discouraged thinking they are trying so hard, yet they are so far off the path of God. But you must look at how far you have traveled and that you have come a long way. If you ask God, I am doing good, am I not Lord? God will say, very good my child. You no longer have to look back, keep your eyes forward into the light until you enter my Kingdom. God is very patient."

They were still walking on the rocky path. It was a steep sandy embankment on the left side; with patches of weeds, grass and small brush growing here and there going down about 50 to 60 feet. They were heading towards a grassy area and then the tree line started again. Ajh continued, "Now let us move on to another commandment, "*Love thy neighbor as thyself*." This is very important, one because it covers everything with your behavior with other people."

Just then a loud roar came from behind them. "What now" with an expression of annoyance on Ajh's face. Coming at them was a huge grizzly bear. Shela screamed as John started pushing her to run towards the tree line then pushed her up a pine tree. Ajh started walking towards the bear. By this time Shela and John were up the tree. John looked at Ajh, "He is crazy!" They watched Ajh standing in front of the bear, as the bear reared up on his hind legs to strike at Ajh. Shela covered her eyes, "I can't look." John turned his head and closed his eyes.

There was a sound like a scuffle, then silence. Shela said, "my God, what happened to him?" John said, "I don't know." He slowly turned his head and peaked with one eye, "I don't see him, oh, there he is. I don't believe it!" She said, "What's the matter, is he all chewed up?" He shook his head, "no, look!"

She turned her head slowly and opened her eyes; and could not believe what she saw. There was Ajh at the bottom of the hill sitting on the bear's belly, talking to the bear. They climbed down the tree and started walking down the hill. The bear spotted them, he roared and got up knocking Ajh over and chased after them. They started running back up the hill. Ajh yelled, "Be still," the bear stopped and sat down.

Ajh climbed up the hill toward the bear. They walked back to Ajh. She asked, "How did you do that?" Ajh shook his head, "you are not listening to me, are you? Anything is possible through God." John said, "Are you going to tell me you knocked him down!?" Ajh answered, "Well it is not impossible, but that is not what happened. When he reared up on his hind legs to strike at me, he was almost on top of me when I said, be still. He tried to stop his attack. I lost my balance and grabbed his fur. He stepped on some lose rocks and lost his footing. With my weight pulling on him, we fell and rolled down the hill, I just hung on to him, it is a good thing I ended up on top."

Shela said, "Look at him." The bear was sitting down, looking up at them, as if listening to what they had to say. "He's like a little puppy." Ajh said, "Go ahead, and pet him." She went over to the bear without hesitation. John was nervous, "Shela watch it. You don't know what." Ajh interrupted, "there is no need to worry he knows he is among friends."

"John questioned Ajh with a condescending voice, "how can a bear know something like that?" Ajh answered, "I know, he has the brain the size of a walnut, but when God speaks everyone listens. The bear feels peace and serenity he has never felt before and he likes it. Look at him." Shela was scratching his head and feeling his fur, talking to the bear. Ajh continued, "If man would turn to God and do his will, the whole world would be like this, in peace and in harmony with the animal kingdom and mankind. There would truly be peace on earth." Ajh looked around him. "It is a beautiful world. We need to stop an enjoy it."

They walked up the hill into the shade where the trees were dense and the bear followed. "Now let's see, I did skip a commandment, I am getting mixed up with all these interruptions. We covered false gods." John asked, "I met some people who were into astrology and they pointed out that in the bible it said God gave the stars in the heavens for signs, is that true?"

Ajh answered, "It does not mean something you believe in or guide your life by but to be able to tell the coming of events. For example, if the sun is going down and it is red, you know it is going to be hot tomorrow. Farmers plant or harvest their crops by the full moon. Or when you see a lot of lightning strikes to the ground, you know that there is going to be an earthquake near the area. And if the stars or planets are in line it could cause problems on Earth, just like sun spots change weather patterns. These are all signs."

"Shela asked, "What do you mean?" Ajh continued, "Well just like in the time of Christ, the three wise men knew a king or savior was going to be born, because of the signs of the times, some people think they studied the stars. In those days a lot of people did believe in the stars. An angel told them to follow one star to Christ. They knew it was time to fulfill the scriptures. All these false beliefs of astrology, numerology and so on came from ancient people from a time when mankind fell away from God. Yet people still believe in them."

"People who believe in astrology claim the stars have an effect like gravitational pull on the tides from the moon. Scientists say that the stars are too far apart for gravity to have an effect on anyone on earth. But gravity is not what is going on here. It is frequency. Scientists know today that everything vibrates at a different frequency, including the planets and stars. Scientists have been able to record the sound of the universe like music. When you listen to different music, you have different moods and your mood affects your day. Your brain also works on a frequency. Your mind is like a receiver and transmitter, this is how telepathy is done. Anyways, these frequencies have an effect on you if you let it, if you believe in astrology."

"There are those who say they believe in God, but everyday they read the newspaper for their sign. They are putting more faith in astrology than in God, so naturally as they see their signs coming true, they believe in it. But in reality, if you look at all the signs, they can all be meant for you. They just switch them around for different days of the month and a lot are just common sense, which a lot of people do not have much of today. If people who believe in astrology read another sign other than there own for about a month and they will find that it still works the same for them, which means it is their own mind that is making it come true."

"Remember only believe in God having an affect on your life, and then nothing else will have an affect on you. The rewards are endless; your life will have guidance and joy that others can not comprehend. Jesus did not want you to worship Him. He wanted you to worship God the Father only and in doing so, the way He did, in His name and you would be giving Jesus great honor. This is why He said, "*I am the door and the way to God.*"

"You can not just read or mimic His words, act them out. Do them and follow in his footsteps. He is the savior that all religions seek. Jesus shed His blood and gave you the word so you could be saved; His words are of the truth. Read the four gospels of the words of Jesus in the New Testament over an over until you do understand. Fill your heart with His words and day to day something will happen that will remind you of a parable He spoke of and you will have a deeper meaning of His words, and you will understand what God expects of you and your purpose in life."

"Everyone has gifts from God. We should use them to help each other. Some people keep their gifts or talents locked up inside of them. Either they do not know what their gifts are or they do not know how to use them. Trust in God, ask him to help you to find and use your gifts so you can fulfill your purpose in life. You could be blessed with more than one gift. The Holy Spirit can bless you with many gifts; all you have to do is ask. Remember, do not try to find ways on how to make money for yourself, but use your gifts to help others and to do God's work, and you will be taken care of."

John remarked, "You mentioned before that people don't have much common sense today, why is that?" Ajh answered, "It is the way people are taught in school today. Kids are allowed to use calculators and computers, there is no problem solving going on in the mind. You see even simple math is very good to exercise that part of the brain to figure out problems. This part of the brain that solves problems in math is also the part of the brain that is used to solve problems in everyday life. Which is what common sense is, solving a problem. Take the calculator away from them and the problem will be solved."

"Look at the people that believe in evolution without reading into the complexity of genes and everything that exist. Just the complexity of how our blood clots and all the chemical changes it takes to do this, that alone is enough to put doubt in evolution. Because the first creature that ever existed with blood would have cut itself and bled to death. And that would have been the end of any creature with blood until, according to evolution it evolved again with some knowledge of blood clotting. This is impossible without God. Do they think this came about by chance? Just a little common sense will tell you that something else must be involved for this to happen. I will talk more about evolution latter."

"A lot of people like to think of themselves as being intelligent yet they do not look objectively into what they believe in, or do research into it. Most people what they believe in comes from what they heard from other people's beliefs, or what they saw on TV or a book and they assume that information is true without looking into it. How intelligent is that?

These people who they believe are giving you intelligent information could also be getting their information second hand and adding their own interpretation and beliefs."

"Even religious people do not look into the Bible to see if what they are being taught by their pastors, priests, rabbis or who ever is teaching them to see if what they say is true. Religious people should also study science and their latest findings so God can give them the true answer. This way there will be another way of looking at the findings not just a scientist point of view."

CHAPTER IV

HOW THE MIND WORKS:
THE TEACHINGS OF OTHER RELIGIONS AND
CONTINUING OF THE TEN COMMANDMENTS

John asked, "If Adam and Eve didn't sin, would we still be living in paradise and have God's power?" Ajh answered, "Yes, in fact, Adam did not realize his full potential before he had sinned. For example, God sent all the animals in the world to Adam to give them a name. Could any human on earth do that today? And all the animals were friendly with man, like this bear." The bear roared, knocked Ajh over and jumped up and down as if to play. Then Ajh started imitating the bear, rolling his shoulders, jumping up and down on all fours. Ajh looked funny and it made them laugh.

They continued climbing to the top of the hill. They were exhausted as they came to a cool shady spot under some pine trees. There were lots of soft pine needles to sit on. The bear lied down and Ajh leaned against him, as if using the bear as a soft chair. Shela asked, "What was Adam and Eve's sin that we should be punished so badly for?" Ajh said, "Hold on a minute, God is not punishing you. He punished Adam and Eve, and you are punishing yourselves." They looked puzzled and shrugged their shoulders. "What do you mean, how?"

Ajh answered, "Adam and Eve sinned by not obeying God and by thinking that the material world had much to offer. To this day, mankind still acts and thinks the same way. Each generation passes its sins and beliefs to the next generation becoming further away from God. Until you have an adulterous and immoral generation of people, that look for objects and stars to guide their life. If you truly believe in God, then only seek God for guidance and help. Jesus was here to show you a path toward God, to lead you away from your sins. He shed His blood so you would know the truth."

"Christ spoke of this generation and this is the time he will come again. God has punished mankind from time to time, but people did not learn then, and it does not seem they will learn anything today. God cast them out of the Garden of Eden, destroyed Sodom and Gomorra, and warned Noah of the great flood. He sent messengers and His Son, still no one listens."

John asked, "Could eating a fruit give us knowledge?" Ajh answered, "Science is discovering that certain chemicals in plants go right to certain parts of the body and glands. Well the Tree of Knowledge opened the gland, and the door of understanding of good and evil. Just as the Tree of Life would have made us immortal by keeping the gland continuously working instead of shutting down as we come to our adult age."

"When God saw that the sons of God found the daughters of men fair, He reduced their age to 120. Yet they still continue their adulterous ways." John asked, "Then why do people die at 60 or 70?" Ajh answered, "Well, as we grow up we look at people in their 70's and say they are old and that is what we will look like at that age. Your mind becomes programmed to start aging when the time is right. You believe without doubt that by the time you reach 70 you will have wrinkles, aches and pains that come with age."

"From the beginning you say how old you are, not how young you are, always on the negative thinking. Then you talk to people with arthritis and rheumatism; the list is endless. As your mind dwells more and more on these aging disease, the more they grow in your system. Your subconscious does not know right from wrong and because your thinking is steadily on a disease, your subconscious changes the chemistry to produce the infection or disease you are thinking so much of. It is written in the bible, "*The thing I feared most has come true.*" Of course our way of life with poor air quality and all the chemicals in our bodies does not help.

John said, "I don't know when I am going to die." Ajh continued, "maybe not, but when you approach that age you will be saying things like, I do not have long now, or I will not reach 80, and you will talk more and more about your aches and pains. The more you talk the worse they get. That is one reason why Jesus said, "*Let anything that comes out of your mouth be yes, yes, or no, no and anything else is evil.*" This is true because you are subject to what you say all the time. And it also eliminates idol talk and gossip"

"Like I said your subconscious part of the mind is like a computer, it does not know right from wrong. It fills your memory banks with all the information of everything you think, say, and do, and whatever your conscious mind reasons to be true. Then it feeds this information back to you when you make decisions. This is what makes up your personality."

"Even when you are joking around, it is stored in your subconscious as something you believe. So when you tell sick or prejudice jokes, eventually you become what you think is so funny. The subconscious is a very delicate and powerful part of the mind. Yet we toy with it like it means nothing. There are more secrets within than there is without."

"Subliminal advertising is something man uses a lot of today without thinking of the consequences. People have no idea how dangerous it is. And most of the public does not know anything about it. Part of their technique is slow brain washing, with hidden messages that the subconscious mind can see and hear but your conscious mind can not. The messages are targeted right to the subconscious, messages of sex, death, oral sex, homosexuality and anything else they can think of to sell their products. That is why a lot of scenes are flashed on the screen to go right to the subconscious. Even children's cartoons are done this way. A good way to see what they are doing is to tape commercials or a show. When you play it back in slow motion you will see usually sexual implications.

"The bible has no hidden messages, it has words of deep meaning that take time to understand. It seems odd when you hear people say that a prophet in the bible was just an ignorant Shepard or farmer that made up stories about their lives and what went on around them. Yet all the wisdom originally came from the prophets in the bible. Archeologists use the bible to find ancient lost cities. Would they even have a clue where to look if it was not for the Bible and the scriptures? The true meaning of love can be found in the words of Christ and his actions."

"Even when I was an atheist, I thought of the bible as a source of wisdom. And the right way to live as a society, would be to follow the Ten Commandments. I also believed in life after death, my experience with leaving the body in spiritual form proved that the soul can live outside the body. But I did not believe in God; that a being, could control the universe. Little did I know of the truth."

Shela asked, "You were an atheist?" Ajh answered, "Yeah, I was for about ten years. I considered myself an intelligent person. I did not accept the theories on evolution, not even my own theories until I could prove them. But there was always a missing link, it just did not add up. The odds were staggering against any life form to develop, with all its complexities, let alone the number of different life forms that are on the planet past and present. I studied religions, how the mind works, astrology, astronomy, metaphysical, and so on. All my studies lead me back to God, and with God's help I began to understand Him. As I looked back on my life I saw that God was guiding me the whole time."

"It was God the Father that chose me to be a reborn Christian. And God began to show me how He feels, wants, and expects of us, and most of all, how much love He has for us. You two are here with me learning about God and you do not know why. I did not know why He chose me either, but now I do. As you open your mind and heart to God, He will grow inside you like a mustard seed, until you are a tree of His life and you become part of Him."

Ajh was silent for a few minutes, so they could think about what he said. It was quiet, you could hear the wind blowing, the birds chirping, the chipmunks running around the rocks, and the bear snoring.

Shela asked, "What did you do before?" Ajh answered, "Well, when I was 12 I worked in my dad's store repairing appliances, when I turned 16 I started working on golf courses. In high school I took up electronics, but went to college for Turf Management at U Mass. I was an assistant superintendent on a golf course in New York and another one in N. Providence R.I.. Then I was drafted, returned to golf course work, and landscaping, I became a foreman for a tree company trimming trees for the electric company. Owned and managed a convenience store for eight an half years. I drove tractor trailer throughout New England, I had a chemical license and was a lawn specialist for over 10 years. I also was a musician and composer and I wrote children stories." Shela was taken back a little, "Wow, you were into everything!" Ajh answered, "Yeah, the Holy Spirit has blessed me with many gifts. My mother use to say I was "a jack of all trades, master of none." But I finally found a trade I enjoy more than all the others, and it feels good."

Ajh continued, "now where was I, I do get off the subject. They nodded their heads, Shela said, "I'm hungry." John remarked, "me too, those berries didn't hit the spot." Ajh said, "Well okay, but it is better that you learn to fast and pray or meditation will also help, because it is good for your body and your spiritual well being. Later just the words of God will fill you and you will no longer hunger or thirst."

Shela asked, "How does fasting help the body and soul?" Ajh explained, "Well first it helps the body by allowing the body to cleanse itself. Your body is overloaded with impurities this is where most of the illnesses come from. Every day you eat more impurities than your body can filter out. So fasting gives your body time to cleanse itself. At the same time, by fasting, you are not pleasing the senses. Your body slows, and calms down, your spirit becomes more peaceful and quiet, and in prayer or meditation you are more in tune with God."

"When you meditate, by slowing the body and calming the mind your brain wave frequency comes down and the voltage in the mind increases. The lower the frequency the higher the voltage. When there is higher voltage in the brain, this is when ESP, Telepathy and other capabilities are possible. When you are awake like now, your brain wave frequency is about 18 to 24 cycles. When in deep meditation you can bring it down to 6 or lower. When you practice this often, then in your waking state you will be at 18 cycles and lower, which means you will be calmer and have more intelligence. Unless you hype your self up with caffeine or nicotine or any thing else that agitates your body." John said, "I'm still hungry."

Ajh stood up and walked behind the tree. He came out with three loaves of bread. Shela asked, "Where did you get the bread?" Ajh smiled, "Behind the tree, you did not see me walk over there?" She laughed, "You know what I mean." Ajh smiled, "from God." John asked, "I noticed you didn't have the Bible with you before, then when the sheriff came you had one in your hand, and what did you do with it?" Ajh answered, "God gives me what I need when I need it, and then takes it away when I am through. It helps not having to carry everything around with me. Ajh sat down by the bear, breaking the bread, giving some to them and said, "Let us give thanks to our Father, who art in Heaven for the bread we are about to eat, we do this in memory of Jesus Christ our Savior, Amen." They started to eat and the bear woke up smelling the bread, so Ajh gave the bear a loaf of his own.

Ajh continued, "Doing the will of God and you will be closer to Him. You will find it easier to fast, which will calm the body and spirit and becoming closer to God. You will get deeper into meditation in a spiritual way. Give your heart and soul to Him. That will be your greatest treasure in Heaven. You will know what God wants from you. Search inside your heart, the answer is there, because that is where God is. Not everyone is meant to preach, which is what many people think they should be doing. But everyone is different; there are many gifts from God. Most treasures are saving souls to enter Heaven. Most religions teach of ways to help each other and to do God's will. But the message should be how to be caring, loving and understanding to all people of all religions. Listen and I will teach you the basics of the most popular religions."

Islamic Teachings and Truths

Islam means, submission to the will of God. Muslim is derived from, one who submits. Islam is a brotherhood of men under God, transcending barriers of race and nation, united in an organized effort to execute God's will. They also follow many scriptures of the Bible.

1

The likeness of those who spend their wealth in Allah's way has the likeness of a grain which grows seven ears and in every ear one hundred grains.

2

Where as the life of the world is but a brief comfort as compared with the hereafter.

3

Allah says, "Who so ever has true knowledge of the scriptures is sufficient witness between Me and you."

4

He who rejects false deities and believes in God only, has grasped a firm hand hold which will never break.

5

A kind word with forgiveness is better than almsgiving followed by injury.

6

The devil promises destitution and lewdness, Allah promises you forgiveness with bounty.

7

Allah loveth not aggressors.

Righteous is he who believeth in Allah, and the Last Day, and the angels, and the Scripture, and the Prophets; and giveth his wealth, for love of Him, to kinsfolk, and to orphans, and the needy, and the wayfarer and to those who ask, and to set slaves free; and observeth proper worship and payeth the poor-due. And those who keep their treaty when they make one, and be patient in tribulation and adversity and time of stress. Such are they who are sincere. Such are the God fearing.

Chinese Precepts

1

Those who, when young, show no respect to their elders, achieve nothing worth mentioning when they grow up.

2

Never do to others what you would not like them to do to you.

3

When the way prevails in the land, be bold in speech and bold in action. When the way does not prevail, be bold in action, but conciliatory in speech.

4

Just as lavishness leads to presumption, so does frugality to meanness, but meanness is a far less serious fault that presumption.

5

He that is really good can never be unhappy.
He that is really wise can never be perplexed.
He that is really brave is never afraid.

6

It is goodness that gives to a neighborhood its beauty.

7

If you hurry things, your personality will not come into play.
If you let yourself be distracted by minor considerations, nothing important will ever get finished.

8

If you were only free from desire, thieves would not steal even if you paid them to.

9

You may rob the Three Armies of their commander-in-chief, but you cannot deprive the humblest peasant of his opinion.

10

Often times one stripes one's self of passion in order to see the Secret of Life.
Reaching from the Mystery into the Deeper Mystery is the Gate to the Secret of All Life.
Tao is Great, the Heaven is great, the Earth is great, the King is great.
The Tao that can be told of is not the Absolute Tao.
Life springs into existence without a visible source and disappears into infinity.

Buddhist Doctrines

Enlightenment on a path toward God.
These are the noble eight fold paths.

1.	Right view	5.	Right means of livelihood
2.	Right intent	6.	Right endeavor
3.	Right speech	7.	Right mindfulness
4.	Right conduct	8.	Right meditation

9

We are the result of what we have thought.

10

Seek salvation alone in the truth.

11

If a man speaks or acts with a pure thought, happiness follows him like a shadow that never leaves.

12

The faults of others are easily perceived, but that of ones self is difficult to perceive.

13

If a man foolishly does me wrong, I will return to him the protection of my ungrudging love.

14

All desires should be abandoned, but if you cannot abandon them, let your desires be for salvation, that is the cure for it.

15

Shame on him that strikes, greater shame on him who when stricken strikes back.

16

All that we are is the result of what we have thought.

Whoever gives alms which do not harm others, His resulting pleasures will never be carried away by water, nor burn by fire, nor stolen by thieves.   Such possessions will never be utterly destroyed.

Hindu Beliefs

Believe that God or Brahman is part of all of us. They believe that spirituality means to return to the spirit. Believe that among the millions of gods there is one supreme God. They also believe that the words of Jesus are true. They do not see time as an arrow or a flowing river but as a pool of water. At intervals there are waves or ripples in the pool; the pool itself remains unchanged.

1

The limbs become pure by water.
The mind becomes pure by truth.

2

Man is the creator of his own fate.

3

Only virtue and good deeds endore.

4

Aspirants may find enlightenment by two different paths for the contemplative is the path of knowledge.
For the active is the path of selfless action.

5

He who longs for God, finds him. Go and try for three consecutive days with genuine earnestness and thou art sure to succeed.

6

The sunlight is one in the same wherever it falls, but only bright surfaces like water or mirrors can reflect it fully. So is divine light, it falls on all hearts, but only the pure and clean hearts of the good and holy can fully reflect it.

7

He whose mind is always fixed on God requires no other practices, devotion, or spiritual exercises.

8

Wound not others , do no one injury by thought or deed, utter no word to thy fellow creatures.

9

True happiness is born of self reliance.

10

One should speak truth and speak what is pleasant.

The Law of Judaism

Life is not a burden to be escaped, but God's gift to be lived fully according to his will. In Jewish religion the home is the center of Jewish faith, equal with the synagogue as a house of God. To raise a family with loyalty is a sacred duty to Judaism. They also follow the Ten Commandments and teachings of the Old Testament and Moses. Here are some of their sayings.

1.   He who advertises his name looses it.
2.   He who does not increase knowledge, diminishes it.
3.   He who refuses to learn, merits extinction.
4.   He who puts his talent to selfish use, wastes away.
5.   The world is established on three things, on law, on worship, and on generosity.
6.   The creator, is not a body, in that he is free from all the properties of matter, and he has not any form whatsoever.
7.   If I am not for myself, who will be, but if I am only for myself, what am I?
8.   Repent before it is too late.
9.   Be avid to learn the Torah and know how to refute a disbeliever.
10. Man doth not live by bread alone, but by everything that proceedeth out of the Lord doth man live.
11. Believe that to the Creator, Him alone is the right to pray, and is not right to any other being besides Him.
12. Believe that the Creator rewards those that keep His Commandments and punishes those that transgress them.
13. Believe with perfect faith that the whole Torah, now in our possession, is the same that was given to Moses our teacher.

They are also waiting for the Messiah; they believe Elijah will announce the coming of the Messiah on the Passover. Adam's fall is not seen as a stain passed on, but rather as a fault repeated because of man's weakness. They also believe that there will be a revival of the dead at the time when it should please the Creator, blessed be His Name, and exalted be His fame for ever and ever. For thy salvation I hope, O Lord.

Christianity

Believe in God the Father, Jesus Christ the son, and the Holy Spirit.
That God raised Jesus from the dead.
Believe in the Ten Commandments.
Most Christians believe Mary was a virgin for the birth of Jesus.
These are some of the teachings of Jesus Christ.

1

Love thy neighbor as thyself and love God with all your heart and soul, are the two most important commandments which all of the rest of the Law is based on.

2

If you are angry with any person, you are guilty before God.

3

Make friends with your enemies before you ask God for forgiveness of your sins, and pray for those who persecute you.

4

If someone sues you for your shirt, let him have your coat also.

5

If someone slaps you on your right cheek, offer him your left cheek.

6

If you love those who love you, what reward have you, do not even thieves do the same.

7

If you can not forgive anyone of doing wrong to you, then God will not forgive you of your sins.

8

No one can serve two masters, you cannot serve God and mammon.

Do not worry about food or clothing. The birds do not worry and they are fed. And the lilies are clothed better than Solomon. You are worth more to God then flowers and birds, but seek first the Kingdom and righteousness of God and all these things will be added.

10

Do not take the splinter out of your brother's eye until you have taken the log out of your eye.

11

The lamp of the body is the eye, if therefore your eye is single, then your whole body will be full of light.

12

Be perfect as your Father in Heaven is perfect.

13

Man shall not live on bread alone, but on every word that proceeds out of the mouth of God.

14

You are all my brothers and sisters who do the will of God.

15

If you have faith as a mustard seed, you shall say to this mountain throw thyself into the sea, and it shall be done, and nothing shall be impossible to you, but this kind does not go out except by prayer and fasting.

16

I say to you, unless you are converted and become like children, you shall not enter into Heaven.

17

If your eye causes you to stumble, pluck it out and throw it from you, it is better you enter life with one eye then having two eyes to cast into the hell fire.

18

Anyone who looks upon a woman with lust has committed adultery with her in their heart.

Jesus also spoke when he will come again and the end of time.
1. It will be a time of an adulterous generation.
2. There will be wars and rumors of wars.
3. Great earthquakes in diver's places and famine and pestilence.
4. You will be hated by all nations on account of my name.
5. Many false prophets will arrive, misleading many.
6. Because of lawlessness is increased, most people's love will grow cold.
7. This gospel of the Kingdom shall be preached in the whole world for a witness to all nations, and then the end shall come.

8. You shall see the abomination of desolation which was spoken of through Daniel, the prophet.

9. Brother will deliver up brother to death, a father his child, and children will rise up against parents and cause them to be put to death.

"All this sounds like this generation, does it not? It sounds like all the things that are happening today and the past. Jesus said this generation will not pass till all these things are fulfilled. He was speaking of the generation that saw two world wars, all the conflicts, the way we have strayed away from God. And this generation is coming to an end."

"Jesus said to do the will of the Father. That was the basics of His whole teachings. All words of wisdom can be found in the bible and in the words of Christ which come from God. As you can see, all religions have truths of God, and are very much alike in their basic teachings. And the bible, has influenced all religions, there are many similarities. Even if they do not believe in God the Father, their teachings follow the basics of the Ten Commandments."

"It is in the writings and teachings that are not from God that man differ in opinion. If you do God's will the best you can, doing what Jesus said to do, when you die God will hold your soul in his hand and will say you have a ton of treasures in Heaven and only a pound of sin. Take this sin and throw it into the fire. And come with me into my house and I will call you my child. Your rewards of your faith are unimaginable."

"People are convinced that earth is hell. Yet compared to hell, this is paradise. They worry about their life now, but their life is but a blink of an eye compared to eternity. Strive for rewards that are beyond your imagination. Have faith in God."

"I will give you an example on how strong your faith should be. A rich man comes up to you and you are out of work. He says to you come work for me and I will pay you good wages. So you go and work for him. Now there are a lot of people working in the field, but some workers began to quarrel saying, why are we working so hard, we do not know what he is going to pay us. How do we know it is worth this hard labor? So they went to the rich man and said, we think you are taking advantage of us, we quit. The man lead them to the gate and paid them. They began to cry out, begging him to let them back to work. The man turned and said, you wanted out because the labor was hard and you had no faith in me. You have been paid your just reward."

"Now about the ninth hour you said to the man, I have had enough, I am tired. So he leads you to the gate and pays you. You realize he paid you $100 an hour. The man said, "On the 12th hour I start paying $1,000 an hour and it multiplies after that." So you ask him to let you back in. He says, no, you grew tired of the work and you only want to work now because you know of what you will receive in return, not because it is in your heart to labor for me. You have your just reward. Blessed are those who labor until they fall asleep. And in the morning they wake up and continue to labor without question. Because in their hearts is faith in me, knowing I will take care of them. They shall inherit my kingdom."

Shela and John were listening very attentively. Ajh continued, "It will be the same with God. Labor for him until your skin wears off your bones. Do not worry about food or clothing. But fill your body with the Holy Spirit of God, and when your body perishes your soul will be in God's hands and you will say, I am in such joy I should have labored even harder. Because you will be rewarded according to your labor for God."

Shela asked, "What do we do to labor for God? Is that the same as treasures in Heaven?" Ajh answered, "Yes it is, labor and do His will. First ask God for forgiveness of your sins, do away with materialistic things, possess and desire nothing of this world, do away with pleasing of the senses. Do things that are of God, like helping people and receiving nothing in return. Judge no one, love everyone as if they are the closest person to you, even the people that hate you, help bring them to God. And most of all give God the credit for all the good you do. If you can do any four of these, you will be close to God and you will begin to understand the reason for doing the others, so you can be closer to Him. If you ask Jesus it will be much easier."

John asked, "Bringing people to God, you mean to preach to them?" Ajh answered, "Well more like following the path of Jesus preach openly. Let them come to you, that way their ears and hearts are open. Preaching is not the only answer, like I said before; you have and can receive many gifts from God."

"Find out what your gifts are. If you have more than one gift, fulfill them for God's purpose. It could be something you are doing now and do not know it. If you care for the elderly or handicap, make them happy bring them joy. If you sing or play an instrument, play for God. Make the words in your music a message from God to the people. And if you receive money for what you do, then help the poor, the starving, and homeless. Do good as your Heavenly Father does good for you. You will be rewarded."

"But there will be some that will ridicule you to harden the hearts of others. Do not let it bother you when laughter and ridicule is their way of trying to get to you, they want you to join them because they are weak. Misery loves company. Learn to have wisdom, when to speak and when to be silent. God will send the Holy Spirit and tell you what to say. Because if you argue with them, they will walk away angry and say things they did not mean, and you will have accomplished nothing. If you accept God as your guidance, he will fill you with the Holy Spirit, and you will have wisdom that no one will be able to question. Let God speak through you."

Shela said, "You never finished the Ten Commandments." Ajh answered, "oh yeah, I do get off the track. Let's see, well one that is very important, *"Love thy neighbor as thyself."* The more you love others, it would eliminate greed, selfishness, poverty, prejudice, and all forms of ignorance. And as you spread love, you will see the health and welfare of the world getting better and it will be a much happier place to live."

"And loving thy neighbor does not mean just your close friends or relatives, or the person next door. Love everyone equally; even people you do not know, or the ones that hate you, love them all like they are your closest relatives. By obeying this commandment, it will be easier to follow the rest, and if you put the feelings of others first and yourself last you will understand Jesus and you will see God the Father."

"One commandment that many young have broken today is, *"Thou shalt honor thy mother and thy father."* Many today do not respect any of their elders. Remember the Chinese Precept saying "Those when young have no respect for their elders, they will not grow up to be anything worthwhile", and this is true. It does not mean that you have to agree with everything your parents say or do. But do not argue with them, have respect, just be silent. This will help you in learning to deal with the world and others in life, it will teach you humility and you will become a better person."

"Shela, your name is spelled S-H-E-L-A, why?" She answered, "Because my mother was not very intelligent and she couldn't spell very well, and that is the way she spelled it on my birth certificate. Ajh asked, "Even though your teachers kept correcting you?" Shela said, "Yes, because I love my mother very much and it makes me feel good to remember her that way, it was part of her. I wasn't going to change the spelling." Ajh said, "That is what the commandment means. You love and respect them no matter what."

John asked, "And what about when parents abuse their children, what should the child do then?" Ajh answered, "That child should seek help and the parent needs help also. And if the children have to leave their family, then leave to people who can help them and in turn help their parents. But you do not hate your parents. There is something that went wrong in the parent's life or something that went wrong mentally. Do not follow their mistakes or their footsteps with hatred and abuse as a way of life, or you could end up just like them, and do the same to your children. Have love and compassion in your heart. Find the right path toward God."

"The next commandment, *"Thou shalt not kill."* This is obvious, but people do not understand that calling for the death penalty, or killing in a war, or having an abortion, you are still breaking the commandment. And do not kill one's spirit by belittling them. It takes much wisdom to do things against society's way of thinking so you do not break God's Laws. Also by lying and gossiping you are breaking the commandment, *"Thou shalt not bear false witness against thy neighbor,"* because they can be scarred for life. Many people are guilty of this today in gossiping about others, even if what you are saying is true. You do not know the whole story and you are still spreading ill will toward that person. Look how many sue with false claims just for the sake of money, or falsify evidence for their own benefit. Anything that is not of the truth is not of God."

"Thou shalt not covet thy neighbor's goods." Or *"Covet thy neighbor's wife."* This has to do with desiring what belongs to your neighbor, and the wanting of materialistic objects. To covet or desire another man's wife, and *"Thou shalt not commit adultery,"* these are grave sins against God. Jesus said, *"Any man that looks upon a woman with lust has committed adultery with her in his heart."* Many people are guilty of adultery in their hearts. Even if you dress provocatively, you are putting lust in another person's heart. And look how many people lust after their movie stars and most of them are married. If adultery is in your heart, there is no room for God."

John asked, "What exactly does adultery mean?" "Well", Ajh answered. "The commandment defines it as having sex with a married person. But according to God, a sexual act between a non-married couple means they should be bonded. Science needs another 20 or more years to discover the health reasons to be celibate before marriage. Even married couples should not take sex lightly."

John asked, "What about all the couples that live together? Religions say they are living in sin. Is that true?" Ajh answered, "That would depend on the couple. Let's say one couple love each other and stay together no matter what happens. God has bonded them. But they should get married, not because man thinks they should, because God wants them too. Another couple may live together only because it is convenient and the great sex they are having. Until they get tired of each other and split up at the first signs of problems in their lives. They feel free because they were not married; they go and find another mate. Now they are living in sin. But do not be self-righteous and judge them or it will be you that is living in sin."

"Sex is not something to take lightly. Satan has put into people's minds that sex is part of life and it is okay. If it feels good, do it. And how could it be wrong if you are not hurting anyone. But if people would open their eyes and look around, they would find a lot of problems associated with this sex revolution they are going through. The rapes, child molestation, disease, pornography that caters to the ignorant, child pornography, people having sex with animals, when and where does it stop? And the divorces, people cheating on each other, because of all the free available sex. How many fall in love because of the great sex they have, then when the sex drive is gone, they find they have very little in common."

"And this is something very important about marriage; it is a bonding of the two. You are not just husband and wife; you are each others best friends. Someone you can trust and confide in with your deepest thoughts and feelings. Someone that is always by your side, always giving you words of love, kindness and encouragement. That is why adultery is a grave sin; you have broken that bond of trust and love. You broke your word too God, that you will be bonded together till death do you part. That is why it is said, the two shall become one. Not one above the other. You are both equal on a journey toward God."

Shela asked, "What did you mean, even married couples shouldn't take sex lightly?" Ajh answered, "making love is something special and beautiful and for raising children. God understands what a young couple is going through," "but", as Ajh pauses, "I know this is hard to understand. If you knew and could feel God and the rewards of his virtues, everyone would keep themselves a virgin. Or we should refrain from sex as often as we can. Because it is of the material world, we must try to live a spiritual life. Remember how pleasing the senses, it keeps you tied to a material world. And Jesus said, "*There is a special place in heaven for those who keep themselves virgins for God.*" We must learn to think spiritually."

"That is what really gets me angry, Satan convincing people that Jesus married someone and having a child. It is all a lie. He never married or had sex. That is what it means to truly follow God. His teachings were of a way to follow God in spirit. It is only the ignorant that believe that everyone wants to have sex. The people, who talk, write books or movies about Jesus marrying and having children are doing Satan's bidding. They are bringing the esteem and level of ideals people have for Jesus down. This way it will be easier for others to say he is not the son of God, but an ordinary man."

"If you are a good Christian, you would not read these books or watch these movies because you know the truth. But they are making a lot of money degrading Jesus and that is all they care about. Stop Satan in his tracks. Do not listen to their lies or acknowledge it. If they go in the hole and loose a lot of money, they will stop."

"There are many heads of religions that do not have sex or marry, so why listen to them when they try to degrade Jesus. There is a special place in Heaven for those who are virgins and if Jesus married and had children, then that means even Jesus cannot go there. They are telling you that the Son of God cannot go to this special place in Heaven because he is not a virgin."

"You see what I mean. These people do not understand God or Jesus. And they cannot even keep their stories straight, some say he had a son and others say he had a daughter. So do not acknowledge their lies. Maybe when they loose their shirt trying to produce these lies, they will quit." Ajh pauses and shakes his head. But even if they loose, Satan wins because of the number of people that believe in these lies and they will spread the word to degrade Jesus because all Satan wants to do is bring as many people with him to hell on judgment day."

"Jesus was trying to show you a spiritual path toward God, the Father. A journey of enlightenment that will open your eyes to the truth. As your eyes become opened your heart will be softened and you will see that all people on Earth are your sisters and brothers."

"You will be able to see the evil that is upon the world, even in the little things that take you away from God. And you will see why you must proclaim your faith to others to open their eyes and if they do not listen to you then you walk away from them. Even if they are your loved ones because either they will laugh at you or they will put sorrow in your heart continuously and possibly you will loose faith. That is why Jesus said, *"Whosoever will not receive you, nor hear your words when ye go out of that house or city, shake off the very dust from your feet for a testimony against them. Verily I say unto you, it shall be more tolerable for the land of Sodom and Gomorrah in the Day of Judgment, than for that city."* You see if people refuse to listen to words of truth then you can not save them. Their life is a lie and confusion and their eyes will never be opened. But maybe when you walk away and they see you will not have anything to do with them, this will soften their heart. And maybe they will come to you and listen. Learn to have wisdom that God has given you. God will give you the words to say to change their heart, let God fill you with His Holy Spirit."

CHAPTER V

IS GOD MALE OR FEMALE:
THE DIFFERENT LEVELS OF HEAVEN
WHAT HELL IS REALLY LIKE

Shela asked, "Tell me, why in the bible everything refers to man and not woman?" Ajh answered, "That is a good question, and there are several answers. First, man gave the spiritual guidance in the family back then. Second, he kept records of what went on. Third, man maintained a spiritual contact with God. Almost all of your prophets were men. Women were more of a materialistic and curious nature that is why they could not resist eating the forbidden fruit. Even today it is mostly the woman that wants a better home, nice yard, a better car, nice clothing always focusing on materialistic needs. Men today are materialistic too, but years ago if you left man alone he would live under a tent in the woods and be happy."

"In most or all religions as they developed into different beliefs, men were the spiritual leaders, while women were subordinate to men. But this is a condition that existed; it is not the way God wanted it to be in the beginning. It is a fact of what existed thousands of years ago and the tradition was carried on."

"God from the beginning created woman from man's rib, meaning she is to be by his side, not beneath him. And the two shall become one. Man is normally the leader because he stays spiritually close to God, and he was not materialistic. But today men have become materialistic and have strayed away from God, so it is up to the woman to lead the family on a spiritual path. It is the ignorance of mankind to try to dominate others to make man feel superior. In a lot of marriages today woman are the spiritual leaders."

"If a woman feels the calling from God to be a preacher of the word then do what He asks, do not wait for others to give you the ok. It does not matter if religious leaders denounce you as a prophetess; do what God wants you to do. Be strong, God is behind you."

"I think it is so petty when people, mostly women, make a big issue of the bible referring to man and not woman. It was written down by man, so what do you expect. They want to rewrite the bible to satisfy those that are ignorant. The bible was written for everyone. They should be more mature to overlook ancient customs and they should look at the meaning of the scriptures. That is what is really important."

Shela asked, "Is God male or female?" Ajh answered, "Well, in your perspective neither. Remember God is pure energy, and the way we look at male and female genders is associated with the physical world, but this is nonexistent in the spiritual world. When you die, you will not have these bodies of male and female. Your bodies will be of pure energy like God. Your personalities will carry on as male and female only, and if you use your body to communicate with people in the physical world, or for what ever reason, then you will use your body as male or female."

"You should call him your Father, because all things come from God. He created you and Mother Nature nurtures you. The same is true in the family, the seed comes from the father and your mother nurtures you in the womb. Therefore you should refer to God as Him. He has a male personality in a spiritual sense. That is why Jesus is a male.

They should not change the words in the bible for these petty ideas. If they worry their minds about little things, then how can they possibly understand the vastness of God? Jesus said, "*He who changes a word in the scriptures will perish in hell.*"

Ajh paused, "now let's return to the commandments I think I skipped, "*Thou shalt not steal*". A lot of people misuse this commandment. They steal from work or from the rich, and they justify their action by saying they are not getting paid enough. Some thieves justify what they are doing saying the insurance company will reimburse the victim. And no one feels bad for the insurance companies. But I tell you this; you will have to answer for every penny before God. On judgment day you will be shown the misery you have caused each person you have stolen from. You would not want anyone stealing from you, so why steal from others. You also should not buy stolen items, because then you are no better than a thief because you are supporting them so they continue to steal."

"Stealing one's pride is also a theft that will not go unpunished, which a lot of people do today with gossip and lies. That is why; "*Love God* and *Love thy neighbor*" are the two greatest commandments which all the Laws of God rest on. We must learn to love each other. God lives within us all. Peace on earth comes from knowing God's ways."

"Let's see, what else can I teach you about the Laws of God?" John interrupted, "Hold it, can we take a break? You don't stop." Shela said, "Yeah, it would be nice to take a break." Ajh nodded his head, "okay, okay. I know I start getting carried away. But I want to explain as much as I can. We will go over this little hill and at the bottom there is a nice spot with a pool of water. So they all got up, Ajh tapped the bear on the belly and said "come on." The bear grunted because he was having a good snooze, then he followed them up the hill.

As they came to the top of the small hill, the sun was going down. After staring for a while into the beautiful scenery and watching the clouds turning colors of red and orange, and finally as the sun set behind the mountains the clouds turned a dark violet color. They started down the hill. Ajh said, "God paints a beautiful and different picture every morning and evening."

Once they reached the bottom of the hill they walked to the stream to get a drink, then walked back to an open area, where they left the bread they carried with them. Ajh suggested too make a campfire. The bear dropped next to the bread and went to sleep. They carried the wood back to where the bear was sleeping, and they put rocks in a circle to make a fireplace. This was about 30 feet from the stream and a small pool that was only about five feet deep. To the right of the pool was another small open area surrounded by trees and some tall grass. Then the hill started going up again about a hundred feet or so.

John was on his knees stacking the wood; searching through his pockets for matches, looked at Shela, "I don't have any matches." Shela said, "Neither do I." John looked up at Ajh, "I suppose you don't have any?" Ajh smiled, "Why do you need matches?" He stretched out his hand over the wood pile and it caught on fire. John's eyes opened wide as he fell back, "Oh, my God!" Ajh replied, "Now you are catching on." Shela laughed, "I love it!"

They picked some berries near the stream then sat by the fire. Ajh was sitting and leaning against the bear using the bear as a backrest. John was on his right and Shela on his left. They all had sticks poking the fire with as they asked Ajh questions about God. John asked, "Ajh, what religion is the closest to God, or the true one?" Shela remarked, "Good one, I bet he has difficulty explaining this one?" Ajh hesitated. Shela said, "Come on, your stalling." Ajh answered, "it is not difficult, none of them." They were surprised by his answer. He continued to explain, "If God were to come on earth, there would be no religions. They all have some truths that are of God, but rituals and ways of man, and they separate themselves from each other. Most religions claim they are the one true religion, and do things that are not of God."

"God gave the Ten Commandments, not as a religion, but as guidance to a perfect way of life. Christ did the same. He showed you a way of life toward God and said do the will of the Father. Jesus was showing you how to return back to God in a spiritual way and how to make yourself perfect as your Father in Heaven is perfect. When we do His will we will become like gods on Earth, sons of the Most High, and we will have His power to do good and He will take care of us."

"All religions put burdens on their people, this is not of God. Some religions make up their own sins. If it is not from God, then how can you say your religion is righteous with God? There are religions that changed the words in the scriptures to accommodate their customs and their own false beliefs. There are very few religions that do all the things that God commanded. Many Christian churches do not do the things that Jesus told them to do, including the prayer, the Our Father, which you very seldom hear in church. We must stop being self-righteous in judging others and look at ourselves and be on a path toward God."

"The heads of most religions are vipers. They burden their people with yokes they themselves cannot carry. How many of them live in luxury, while their people are struggling to get by, or even starving. How many wage war and call it holy, when God said *Thou shalt not kill* and *Love thy neighbor*. Look at the Christian Crusades the blood they spilled and the terrible things they did, this is not of God. And these terrorist that kill in the name of God. This is not the way of Islam. These terrorist should be declared outcast by their religious leaders. Yet they say nothing. If you break God's commandments, then you are not of God. And how can you call it a holy war; that is blasphemy against God. Because there is nothing that is holy except God, or anything that comes from Him."

"The true church is the church of Philadelphia, which is having faith and belief in God and never denying your faith or love for Him. Your heart is the one true church or temple. Let the Spirit of God reside there and you will know the truth."

"I will not say which religion is closest to God, because they will call me a liar and say I favor one over the other. But as long as they separate themselves from each other, they will never know the truth. Judge righteously by that which is righteous. Religions should forget their differences and bring the people together to God. They should put aside their rituals, concentrate on the Ten Commandments, and be on a straight path of righteousness and enlightenment to understand what God wants."

"But I will say this if all religions would add Christ and His words to their religion they would have a clearer understanding on how to do the will of the Father. This does not mean all Christian Religions are right with God. Because there are some that do things against God and do not do His will. What I mean is that by the words of Jesus; from the Four Gospels, will give you the understanding of God's will. Jesus died for us, and shed His blood so that we could be washed of our ignorance of God's way of life. All the teachings of Jesus actually show in depth the meaning of the Ten Commandments. As we follow His path we will see clearer God's intentions for us. Jesus was showing us a spiritual path to take. People should ask themselves why are there so many miracles done in the Christian Faith and only to those that have faith without doubt?

"Now let's get back to the Ten Commandments, *"Thou shalt not kill"* is one even self-righteous people break. They call for war or vote for abortions or the death penalty for hardened criminals. These people are as guilty as those who pull the trigger. The commandment does not make exceptions. When you execute a criminal, he no longer has a chance to tell God he is sorry for his sins, and spends the rest of eternity in hell. Now, the self-righteous are guilty of murder. There is no justification for taking another person's life out of anger, vengeance or as punishment. God did not kill Cain for his brother's death, but sent him away."

"Killing someone's spirit and pride are ways of harming other people and are sins against this commandment, *"Love thy Neighbor as thy self,* and *Do unto others as you would want them to do unto you."* These words are very important to live by."

Shela asked, "How would we deal with other countries that want to take us over and control us?" Ajh answered, "according to the Laws of God and the teachings of Jesus, you become their servants. But remember, if you are totally with God in spirit, they can not harm you nor can they control you, but even to be a servant you can win. A good example was Gandhi, he received his country back without firing a shot or raising his hand, nonviolence was his way. Even when he was struck by the soldiers he offered no resistance, and had no hatred toward them. "

"If we lived by God's Laws and as children of God, you do not need countries, man's laws, boundaries, houses, or religions. If we were with God, the possibilities are endless and beyond our imagination. Think of yourself as pure energy, in the spirit. This is what we were meant to become as children of God and you can not hurt energy, you can not enslave energy. I will explain more about this later. It is difficult to understand when you think of your whole world in a material sense, but you have to learn to think spiritually."

"When Jesus said to turn the other cheek, He was trying to teach you something. If an individual was hitting you and you offered no defense this person would begin to ask himself why? Realizing what he is doing and that he is weaker than you are; you will soften his heart. He might ask you for forgiveness and his heart will be opened and you can teach him about God."

"As for those people that would not settle for another country taking them over, they should build their defenses around their country and just protect themselves. Let the other side waste their resources by attacking. Eventually they will give up. If you do this in the name of God, just to protect your country, God will give you the knowledge to build better defenses so no one could harm you. You would only need a military to protect your borders."

"In all religions, most people figure their preachers know more about the bible and the meaning of the scriptures more so than they do. But these preachers are people with faults and weakness, and they are taught by people with faults and weaknesses. And each one adds their own interpretation and beliefs. Everyone should read the scriptures and ask God to show them what they mean. Always seek the truth. Because God is truth."

Shela asked, "Is that why you quote other religions?" Ajh said, "Yes, there are many truths in all religions. Truth is truth. Religions should try to understand each other, they are very much alike. You must find a church that teaches about spirituality. This is what Jesus was talking about when He said *"You must be reborn into the spirit"* and He said *"When you pray, pray in spirit."* Going to church or the temple should not be a ritual, but a meaningful experience where you go to learn the scriptures and The Commandments to be spiritually closer to God. And these preachers should not be adding their own words to the scriptures or take words out of context to make a point because this is changing the meaning of the scriptures."

They all had sticks and they were poking the coals in the fire. Then Shela stood up to stretch her legs, turned around with her back to the fire. Ajh was poking the fire with his stick when he asked John if he had any questions about God. John didn't answer. Ajh looked at John. He was staring off to Ajh's left. Ajh looked to see what John was looking at. There was Shela bent over touching her toes with skin tight cut offs with her butt hanging out.

Ajh looked at John with a disappointed look and shook his head. He pulled the stick out of the fire and blew on it and said to John, "do you think if elephants had bigger ears, they could fly?" John muttered, "Ah, I guess so" as he kept his eyes on Shela. Ajh took the stick and whacked it across John's chest. John jumped back, brushing off the sparks as they flew off his shirt and yelled, "Are you crazy!? You are out of your mind!! What did you do that for!?" Ajh replied, "Because you are more interested in her butt than what I have to teach you."

Shela turned around and had a coy smile for John. Ajh looked at Shela and said, "I would not be smiling if I were you. You can burn in hell for putting lust into men's hearts just as those who act out their lust." John, still upset, "Look what you did to my shirt!!" Ajh replied, "A stained shirt can be washed or replaced, a stained heart is much harder to replace and can even turn to stone and eventually drag you to the pits of hell."

Shela asked, "How can lust and sex turn you toward hell? If two consulting adults agree to what they are doing, who are they harming?" Ajh shook his head, "You are not listening to me, are you? Do you think there is lust and sex in Heaven?" They both said, "No." "Well" said Ajh, "if sex is in your heart, and all you are thinking about, then your heart is not pure, then how can you enter into Heaven?" *"On earth as it is in Heaven."* Do away with pleasing the senses, pleasures of the skin are not fruitful, they are not of God. To enter Heaven your heart and soul must be pure. I know it is hard to understand and I am not saying all people who have sex are going to hell. But if you could do away with material objects and pleasing the senses, the rewards are beyond your capability to understand. It is like a whole new world of existence."

Everyone now was quiet and staring into the fire. Then Shela asked, "How can you wipe the stains from your heart?" Ajh answered, "Ask God for forgiveness and sin no more." John said, "That's it?" Ajh nodded his head, "yes, and follow his Laws the best you can. But it is a lot easier said than done. Once you learn how to please the senses, it is hard to resist temptation. That is why so many are dragged down to hell and there in between. People say, "Why fight temptation if it feels good." So they go on pleasing the senses and enjoying the world until it is all they want to do and see nothing wrong with it. They no longer think of spiritual matters or of God."

Shela asked, "What do you mean, hell or in between? Is there a place called purgatory?" Ajh hesitated, "well, there are different levels of Heaven, religions call them what they like." Shela asked, "Why are there levels of Heaven?" Ajh answered, "according to your deeds, faith, and love for God, will depend how close you live in God. Those who are purist in heart live in God and God lives in them, they know joy and happiness beyond your understanding."

Shela asked, "What about purgatory, where is that?" Ajh answered, "Well, in the bible and other religions, they all talk about the Heavens with an "s" at the end meaning more than one. Purgatory is a place at the lower levels of Heaven. It is separated because of people who are not pure enough to enter Heaven, but not bad enough to enter hell. And there are people that do not know they are dead, and they continue with their daily lives."

"Some religions have a day they pray for these lost souls; they call it All Souls Day. They pray to God to help and forgive these souls, so they may reach a higher level in Heaven so they may receive peace of mind and rest from their sins. We should all pray for those lost souls to help them into Heaven. Then maybe others will do the same for you when you need it."

John asked, "How long do you spend in the lower levels of Heaven?" Ajh answered, "Well that depends on the individual; how much they repent, pray for their sins and realize where they are and what to do to find God's grace. There are a lot of people who need prayers, but after the judgment everything will be separated into just Heaven and hell."

Shela asked, "What is hell like?" Ajh answered, "You do not want to know." He paused, "There is pain like you could not imagine in hell. You would chew on your own skin." Shela asked, "Why?" Ajh looked at her in the eyes and said, "To cause yourself pain, so you would not feel the pains of hell. There is screaming and horror. Satan constantly drives your worst fears into you and he laughs while you continue in your agony and torture. And there is no water to quench your thirst from the never ending flames."

Shivers went through their spines as Ajh was describing hell. John asked, "How do you know all this?" Ajh answered, "It is written throughout the scriptures and I have experienced it myself."

Shela had a surprised look on her face, "How!?" Ajh continued to explain, "Well before I decided to follow God I had studied many religions and I was shown by God the truth to many things. I realized the only way to follow God properly is to give up all materialistic objects, do away with my ego and self-esteem, humble myself, serve others; in return I will be serving God. Then my eyes will be open and I will see the truth and also see God."

John interrupted, "But how did you experience hell?" Ajh said, "I'm getting to that, be patient. I was a businessman, musician, a trucker, lawn specialist and many other things I like to do. I had a lot of possessions, but I didn't possess them with my heart. To give them up would be easy, but I struggle with the thought, what would my family and friends think of me? And if I did it, would I be accepted by God to do his will?"

"I struggled with these feelings and thoughts for a few years. Finally I had to do it. I could feel a calling inside of me, God wanted me. So I gave up everything and did what Jesus said to do, I gave everything to the poor. Of course, I was ridiculed by family and friends. They said I was a fool for throwing everything away."

"But what I have now, I would not trade for all the treasures on earth. I know now that they are the fools because they cannot see past their material world." John, being impatient, "Well!" Ajh answered, "I'm getting there, so I left with just a pair of jeans, T- shirt, my cross, and sandals. I went deep into the woods; I prayed and fasted for days on end. But still, I felt nothing from God. All kinds of thoughts were going through my head. I said to myself, No, I will not stray from God. He has not abandoned me. I yelled out, Father, I am your son. I beg of you to forgive me and accept me. I claim my rightful place in Heaven. Let me burn in hell to cleanse me of all my unrighteousness, accept me into your heart, as I have you in mine. I give you my heart, my soul, my very existence. Accept me Father. Let me burn in hell to cleanse my soul."

"Suddenly, I was there, in hell. I thought my God, what have I done? I felt pain, pain like torture from heat and fire. It was hard to breath; as the heat burned in my lungs. As far as my eyes could see, I saw fire burning people. I could hear the anguish of people screaming, horrible screams, of fear and pain. I saw people chewing on their own skin acting like mad dogs."

"Then Satan approached me and, as he stood in front of me, I felt something. Like fear from deep inside of me being brought out. I thought I feared nothing, but he found something and magnified it and laughed. I began to shake as the fear grew. Then I realized, as I looked around, that is what I heard in the other people's voices and screams; their pain, their horror, and fear. I was beginning to hate Satan for it. Then I also realized that is what he wanted as he was laughing. Hate is what he thrives on. All those people were filled with hatred of one kind or another when they were on Earth. Some even hated God for being in hell. They should put the blame on themselves and Satan for leading them there."

"I said to myself, I have to be above all this, and to do better. I knew God was watching and feeling my pain because he is a God of compassion. So I looked at Satan, fighting the urge to strangle him, and I said "God ask even you Satan, to turn from your wicked ways and not too lead others astray. Open your stone heart to God, and ask for forgiveness, learn to love and care for others.""

"Everything disappeared; I was out of hell and back in the woods again. I was soaked with sweat and the air felt cold. I remembered the look on Satan's face, to hear the words of love in his own house must have drove him mad with rage. I started to laugh as I thought about the expression on his face."

"Then I started to feel the power of God, love, peace, truth, confidence, wisdom, and all things that are good and righteous. I was truly blessed with the Holy Spirit. As I held my hands against my heart, it was pounding with excitement, I said, "My heart and soul are yours Father! I will do anything you ask of me! Your will is my will! I am grateful for the gifts you have given me!""

Shela asked, "What does Satan look like?" Ajh answered, "He looks like death and all that is evil to drive fear into you. He can change his looks so as to deceive you or fill your heart with temptation." John asked, "What do you mean?"

Ajh continued, "Well, on earth he can look like a beautiful woman to make a man cheat on his wife, or a good looking man to tempt the wife. Look at some of the woman and men today the way they wear their makeup, they do look like Satan's children. Satan could come as an idea to make money, even if it hurts people. He can come as anything that is against God, righteousness and truth to bring you away from God. He can come in many ways and in many forms. Or even posses someone's body to do something evil, it is easy when this person is not of God. You hear Satan in the music of today, the swearing, and all the things that are unrighteous, talking of killings, sex, gangs and blasphemy. These people are so far from God it is easy for Satan to influence them or possess their mind and body."

"Look at the way they talk on the radio, always talking about sex, like they have 12 year old minds, filling your head with lies and telling jokes about God or joking about people with handicaps. Anything that is against God, Satan is behind it. Sex and death is in the movies, even in the kid's video games, and the parents think it is ok. What do you think these kids will be like when they grow up?"

"Satan has influenced people for thousands of years and at a slow pace, so people will not notice how far they have drifted from a righteous path of God. That is what is going on today. People can not see what they are doing wrong, they justify everything they do. And if everyone is doing it, then it must be ok. Satan is here on earth and he is doing his best to take as many souls with him to hell. He knows he does not have much time."

"We must all take a good look at the kind of life we are living and see how far we have strayed from God. We must examine ourselves and everything we do. Do not think it is ok just because the majority is doing it, because the majority is going to hell. That is why everyone must read the scriptures to see for themselves what God wants and expects from us. And if you listen with your heart you will begin to understand God and what He has to offer."

CHAPTER VI

SHELA AND JOHN EXPERIENCE HELL, ARE BAPTIZED AND MARRIED

Shela asked, "Can we experience hell, for a few minutes, so we can be forgiven for our sins?" Ajh answered, "I am glad you said to forgive you of your sins and not what you will gain later. And you John, you are silent." John replied, "Yeah, I guess so. I'm not excited on the idea but I'll do it." Ajh said, "You do not guess so, you have to know." Shela asked, "Can we?" Ajh answered, "Well, it is not up to me. This is very serious. There are a lot of dangers involved, you could."

Suddenly Ajh became silent and his eyes closed. There was silence as they watched Ajh just sitting there, then he opened his eyes and looked at them as he stood up. "God has granted your wish. I must tell you; this will affect you for the rest of your lives. You will look at things differently. Satan will also make you see yourself as you really are, the evil you have done. And he will stop at nothing to drive more fear and horror into you. He will do anything to cause more pain while you are in hell, if possible to drive you insane." Then Ajh stood up and started walking to a clearing.

"One more thing, if Satan should appear before you, do not, I repeat, do not look into his face." "Why not?" asked John. "Trust me" said Ajh. "You could die of shock. His face is the death, the ignorance, the greed, the selfishness, and the horror of all things that are not of God. And he can show you the evil that is in you."

"Stand over there." As he pointed to the clearing, Shela and John stood off to the side in a clearing under the trees, about fifty feet from the campfire and about 30 feet from the stream. They started shaking, there were not sure of what they were getting themselves into. Ajh walked back to the campfire sat down and began to pray.

There was silence, the wind became still, no sound of crickets, frogs or owls even the sound of the rushing water of the stream was silenced. It made Shela and John scared. Then all you heard was a deep whoosh, like the sound gasoline makes when it catches on fire. Shela and John were surrounded by a ring of fire. Flames coming out of the ground lit up the night sky with a reddish-gold color.

They dropped to the ground as if exhausted and began to scream in pain. Shela started pulling at her hair and pounding on her knees as they knelt on the ground. John was punching himself in the chest, and then he started pounding on the ground. Both of them were screaming and crying. Then John started chewing on his finger. Shela started chewing on the skin above her wrist. They were chewing on their skin like a dog tearing at a piece of meat off a bigger piece shaking their heads.

Ajh sat with eyes closed, tears coming down his cheeks, he knew what they were going through. Then there was a scream, a horrifying scream that was worse then the others, it even woke up the bear. Ajh opened his eyes and saw Satan standing in front of Shela in the midst of the fire. Ajh raised his hand and said, "Be gone." Satan disappeared along with the flames.

Ajh ran over to Shela. She was screaming, babbling and drooling. It appeared she was losing her mind. Ajh grabbed her head between his hands as she was struggling to get away; she was crying and mumbling, finding it hard to breathe. He stared into her eyes and said, "Father." Shela began to calm down but continued crying. Tears streaming down her cheeks as he held her face, and she was holding his hands.

Both John and Shela were breathing very heavily from perspiration and body heat. "I told you two not to look at Satan." John answered, "I didn't look at his face. Are you alright Shela!?" Shela answered, "My God, his face was horrible and frightening!" She started crying again, "all those people, their deafening screams, the heat and pain, the whole place was horrible!" John asked, "Why did you leave us in there so long!? We only said for a few minutes!?" Ajh replied, "You were in there for only about 30 seconds. The pain makes it seem much longer."

John, with tears in his eyes and confusion, rubbing his face and hair, the heat was making his face feel prickly all over, "Why hasn't anyone warned people what hell is like!?" Ajh answered, "It is written in the scriptures, but no body pays attention to it. Instead they are convinced this life on earth is hell. Satan has slowly worked into the minds of the people so they do not believe in the scriptures at all. There are false preachers who say there is no hell, and nobody says anything to correct them."

Shela looked at her wrist. "Wow, did I do that to my wrist!?" John said, "Look at my finger!" She looked at Ajh, "Can you take care of it with that healing power you have?" Ajh answered, "It is God's power and we all can use it, but I am going to heal it just a little and let it heal the rest on its own, so it will scar. That way when you look at the scar it will remind you of what you went through tonight." They both were in shock of what they saw and still shaking, "Oh I don't think we'll forget tonight at all!!"

Ajh put his hands over their wounds and said, "There, the bleeding has stopped. Just put some water on, and wash it." Both of them at the same time yelled, "Water!!" They both got up and ran down to the pool of water because they were so hot and sweaty. Ajh ran ahead of them, "No, do not jump into the water! As heated up as your bodies are, the cold water could be quite a shock to you. Just wet your face, and then wet yourself a little at a time until you calm down."

They began splashing themselves and drank some water. Ajh turned and waded into the pool, soaking his robe and then his head. By this time Shela and John had slowly worked their way in, even though it felt cold, everyone was enjoying the water. Then Ajh left the pool and walked to the top of the hill. He stood there a while letting the wind blow through his hair and robe, so they would dry.

When Ajh came down the hill, Shela and John were not by the fireplace. He walked over to the pool of water, they were not there either. Then he heard noise over to his left in the bushes. As he walked over there he could see them making love, and their clothes laid out across the top branches.

Ajh shook his head with a disappointed look on his face. He grabbed their clothes, walked over to the campsite, and threw more wood on the fire to stack the pile higher; rung out their clothes, then threw them into the fire. He sat down and leaned against the bear, which was still sleeping. A few minutes later Shela and John poked their heads out of the bushes and said, "What's burning with all that smoke, what's that smell, and where are our clothes!?" Ajh replied, "The answer to all your questions are your clothes. I am burning these things that create lust in your hearts."

They began yelling at him. "Are you nuts!? What are we going to wear!?" Ajh was silent, poking at the clothes, making sure they were burning, with a smirk on his face. Shela and John were staring at the fire, dumfounded. Ajh looked at them, "Well, are you going to stay in the bushes all night?" John yelled out, "We are naked!" Ajh answered, "God knows what you were doing and you were not ashamed of it!" They looked around, as if to see if anyone was watching them. She yelled out, "What are we going to do!?" Ajh said, "Wait a minute." He got up and walked to a large tree, bent over behind it and picked up some clothes. Walked back to them and gave them the clothes, then sat by the fire.

After they were dressed, they walked over to Ajh. John asked, "Why did you burn our clothes!?" Ajh answered, "I told you, they created lust in your hearts." John said, "I don't think what we were doing was wrong." Ajh replied, "After what I told you about sex?" Shela said, "We were making love." Ajh answered, "really, I did not hear any I love you, instead I heard; Oh John, Oh Shela, Oh John, Oh Shela" as he changed the tone of his voice to match theirs. She said, "Stop that," as her face turned red, and she slapped Ajh on the shoulder.

Ajh was poking the fire with a stick. He looked up at her with a half smile, "Well?" Shela asked, "Well, what?" Ajh asked, "Do you love him?" She answered, "Yeah, yes I love him." Then John said, "Yes, I love her." Ajh asked, "Will you stay with each other for the rest of your lives?" Both of them said, "Yeah, I think so." Ajh looked at them, "you think so? You are supposed to know so." John asked, "How can you know what is going to happen 20 years from now, or even 10?"

Ajh answered, "You know in your heart, even through the hard times, the arguing, the fighting, you know that you will sit down and iron things out, and make it work. You just do not give up after years of working together. If you lose that bondage, then you search in the past, and find where and when you lost it, and ask why. You will find out that most of the time it was for a silly reason or a lack of communication."

"Tell me, are you willing to get married?" "Oh, wow, I don't know" she said. John scratched his head, "Wow that is quite a commitment." Ajh remarked, "Just as I thought, you are phonies. Listen to yourselves, first it is yeah, then I think so, and now it is, I do not know." John said, "Marriage is a serious commitment." Ajh paused and looked at them, "And what you were doing in the bushes is a passing thing?"

They were silent for a while, then Shela spoke up, "I'd be willing to get married" as she looked at John. John put his arms around her, "yeah, me too." Ajh said, "Great, we will have a wedding right now." They were stunned "What, right now, we're not prepared!"

Ajh answered, "What is there to prepare? You both have new clothes. Shela with her off-white ruffled blouse and new jeans, it looks lovely." She said, "I think John looks handsome in his short sleeved white shirt and jeans. But don't you think shorts would be cooler." Ajh answered, "do not worry you will be fine."

"I will be the minister and God will be your witness." They looked at each other and said "okay!" Then Ajh replied, "But first, you two should be baptized in water. Let us go down to the pool of water."

They walked behind Ajh and follow him arm and arm down to the pool. Ajh took off his sandals and walked in about knee deep. He looked at them and said, "Well, come on in." John said, "We'll get our clothes wet. Why can't you do it over here?" Ajh answered, "Get over here. Your skin is waterproof and your clothes will dry. Take off your shoes and walk in."

They waded into the water to where Ajh was standing. Ajh said, "Bow your heads down, so I can pour water on your heads. Remember how to baptize with these words." They bowed their heads before Ajh. He picked up some water and in the sign of the cross, he poured water on their heads, and said, "I baptize thee in the name of love, love of the Father who art in Heaven, love of Jesus Christ, our Savior, and love of the Holy Spirit, the gifts and essence of God, Amen." They put on their shoes and walked back to the fire.

Ajh began gathering small weeds and flowers and made a ring about six inches in diameter, then he put them on Shela's head. She was all excited. John was getting more wood for the fire. The bear just laid there. He threw all the wood on the fire. The flames rose real high as it lit up the woods, the heat felt good, but it was quite strong, they had to back away a little. Even the bear got up to move. Ajh called the bear over and said, "You can be a witness too." The bear grunted and moved over to Ajh, he sat on his hind legs raising his front paw in the air and everyone laughed.

Then John said, "We don't have any wedding rings." Ajh answered, "You have golden rings around your hearts. Rings on your fingers are only to show mankind that you are bonded, but because you will be dealing with mankind in the future, then wear these." As he opened his hand there were two gold rings. Shela and John awed in amazement. She said, "They are beautiful! Thank you! I love the cut leaf in the gold." Ajh said, "thank God, he made them, and they are pure gold, God does not make junk."

They stood together; Ajh in front of them with a bible in his left hand and said, "let us begin. John, do you take Shela as your wife, to be by your side, to love and cherish through sickness and in health, for better or for worse, richer or poorer, to keep in God's ways until death do you part?" John gazed into her eyes, "I do."

"Do you Shela take John as your husband, by your side to love and cherish through sickness and in health, for better or for worse, richer or poorer, to keep in God's ways until death do you part?" She looked into his eyes, both of them with smiles on their faces, "I do."

Ajh continued, "You must remember, God created woman from man's rib, she came from your side and therefore you shall stand side by side, not one above the other, and keep each other close to God. You two are wed by God, let no man separate. The two shall become one, one flesh, one heart." They both put the rings on each other's fingers. "I now pronounce you husband and wife, man and woman, you may kiss." They began kissing. The bear laid down a few feet from the fire and went to sleep.

Ajh started poking the fire with a stick. He turned to them, they were still kissing. "Okay, that's enough, when is it my turn?" He gave her a hug and a kiss on the cheek. Then he gave John a hug and shook his hand, and congratulated them. There was a nice warm feeling in the air. They sat down around the fire. Ajh sat near the bear and leaned against it, using the bear as a back rest. They sat on the opposite side, real close, with their arms around each other. They were both beaming with joy. Shela said, "I feel so good inside!" John said, "Yeah, me too!"

as he hugged her. They talked for a while as Ajh was poking the fire with a stick.

John remarked, as he felt his clothes, "Our clothes are completely dry?" Ajh said, "They were never really wet." Shela remarked, "How is that possible?" Ajh said, "I will give you an example when I was young I grew up in a town called West Warwick, Rhode Island. My dad, Frank, belonged to a club, a Brotherhood that puts on a big feast the three days of Labor Day. The feast would duplicate what the queen of Portugal used to do for her people."

"Well, my dad told me this one particular feast they were visited by a nun. I believe this was in the early 50's. She was one of the three children from Fatima where the Blessed Mother appeared to. My dad said the men were all around her to protect her from the crowd, everyone was pressing to see her. But then, a thunder storm came and it rained very heavily. Everyone ran to the club to get out of the rain. The men tried to push the people aside to help the nun up the stairs because she was very old. But she kept saying, do not worry about me, I will be fine. When everyone was inside the club, they were soaked because it was raining so hard. Then they began to notice that the nun's clothing was completely dry."

"Here is another miracle in my family, I had an Uncle Mike who was going on vacation, but he was having trouble with a soar throat, so he went to see a doctor. When the doctor examined him he found his throat black with cancer and told my uncle that they should start treatment right away. My uncle argued with the doctor that he was going on vacation and will start when he comes back. He was going to Portugal to see my aunt's family and they visited the Shrine at Fatima and he drank the water there. When he returned to the doctor and was examined, the cancer was gone." Ajh paused.

"Here is something I just thought of. When my aunt Mary was dieing, I went visit her in a nursing home. My cousin Pauline and Sheryl were there too. We were talking to each other because my aunt was incoherent, just talking without making sense and mumbling, and her eyes were looking all around. Suddenly her eyes became fixed at the end of the bed at the space between my cousin Sheryl and I and her speech became clear. She said, Jesus you know I love you, take me with you, I am ready, you know I love you; I want to be with you. That knight she died, apparently Jesus was standing at the end of the bed."

"So you see, God is always doing miracles to people that are strong in their beliefs. You just have to open your eyes, mind, and most of all, your heart to God. If you allow God in your life, you can do and see miracles happening all around you. Ask Jesus to help you, He is always there for you."

Shela said, "I'm getting tired." Ajh replied, "Both of you have had quite a day." She answered, "Yeah, one I'll never forget." The fire was starting to lower with a small flame and some hot coals. There was a little silence. Then Ajh said, "Before you go to sleep, I want to show you something. Come over here in the darkness away from the fire."

They sat down in the grass in the opening about 50 feet away with their backs to the fire. Ajh said, "because of the teachings of the world, some people believe in evolution. We'll talk more about evolution later, but what I am pointing out is because of their beliefs, they believe they do not have a soul. This is how you show the disbelievers they have a soul."

"Sit or lie down, make yourself very comfortable in a dark place. Now close your eyes, take a deep breath, exhale slowly, relax, and listen to my voice. You are becoming more relaxed with each breath. Feel all your muscles relaxing, and feeling heavy." Ajh would pause between each statement to give them time to relax."

Ajh continued, "All tensions are leaving your body, you can feel all your muscles becoming relaxed and heavy, as if though you are sinking. Concentrate on each individual muscle from head to toe, becoming more and more relaxed. He paused. Slow down your breathing. Take a deep breath, exhale slowly, and relax."

"Now I want you to stare into your eyelids, keeping the mind free of thought, just like watching TV." Ajh paused to give them time to keep the mind blank. Then he continued, "You will begin to see shadows. This is how ESP begins. The shadows will take form and you will start to see images." They both said, "Yeah, I can see shadows, and their moving around." Ajh continued, "Keep the mind blank, and stay relaxed."

"Focus on the eyelids. Now listen to me very closely. I want you to focus, not on the shadows, but on the light around the shadows. After all, in order to create shadows you have to have light, and where is the light coming from?" John said softly, "I see it, it is getting brighter." Shela said, "Yeah, very bright." They jumped up and said, "Wow, what was that!?" John, was excited, "I started squinting because it was getting so bright, but my eyes were already closed!"

Ajh said, "Do not get upset, and learn to control your emotions and feelings while meditating. That was the light of your soul; it is just a spark of God's light, where we all come from. The spark of our soul that is given to you in the womb, where life begins."

They walked over to the fire and the bear. Shela said, "I'm really getting so tired, that meditation really relaxed me." Ajh answered, "Yes, but never come out of meditation like that, you could have some very strong headaches. Always come out of meditation slowly. Breathe a little faster, move your muscles, stretch them, say out loud and count one, two, and three slowly feeling wide awake. This way you come out of meditation slowly."

"Here is another way you can relax to fall asleep, by stretching your muscles, put out your arms and stretch and twist them. Do this to your back, your neck, your legs, throughout your whole body. When all your muscles have been stretched like this, it is very easy to go right to sleep. You can feel your heart beating a little faster." Shela replied, "Yeah, I can feel it." "Now if you lie back, you'll go right to sleep. And if you do this in the morning when you wake up, it will start your heart beating and you will feel wide awake without needing a cup of coffee. Of course, if you lay back down you might go right back to sleep."

"In the morning, when your heart is beating fast, your blood is circulating, so it makes you feel awake. Well goodnight, you have a long day ahead of you tomorrow." Shela snuggled up against John, and they lay down against each other and went to sleep. Ajh leaned against the bear and went to sleep.

The fire was crackling, popping and dying down. You could hear the crickets all around them, the frogs down by the soothing sound of the rushing water, the peeping of the toads, in the distance you could hear the eerie hooting of an owl, the bear snoring and a wisp of wind through the pine trees. It sounded like a lullaby as they drifted off to sleep.

CHAPTER VII

EXPLAINS WHY JESUS IS THE MESSIAH
THE DESCRIPTION OF HIS CRUCIFIXION
WHAT HEAVEN IS REALLY LIKE

The next morning they all slept a little late, the sun was shimmering through the trees on Shela's face. It woke her, she sat up and stretched and said, "Oh, the air smells so fresh." As she looked over to Ajh she was startled. She shook John and said, "John wake up, wake up, look!" John sat up, rubbing his eyes, and then he gazed over toward Ajh. "Wow, what's going on?"

As Ajh was sleeping against the bear, all around him were other animals sleeping close to him, a deer, mountain lion, fox, rabbit, skunk, and some birds. Some of the animals woke up when they heard Shela talking. Ajh started to wake up. When Shela stood up, the mountain lion showed its teeth, so she sat back down. The cat kept his eyes on them. Ajh sat up and John asked, "Why are all these animals here?" Ajh answered as he began stretching, "They feel the presence of God in me and they want to be close. It is not that they understand, like the bear, they feel secure, safe, relaxed, and comfortable, and they want to be close to that feeling."

Shela asked, "But why a fox and a rabbit, a deer and a mountain lion?" Ajh said, "That is because they have no fear or aggression in them. Their bellies are full, so they are happy and content." She stood up again, and again the mountain lion roared and showed his teeth. Ajh tapped him on the head and said, "No" and then scratched him behind the ears to calm him down.

She asked, "Why is he doing that?" "Because he is not sure about you. He does not sense the same feeling from you as he is getting from me. Come here, he will be alright once he knows you." She walked right over to the cat, feeling confident in Ajh's words. She began petting him and scratching him behind the ears. Obviously the cat loved it as he closed his eyes and tilted his head, and then he leaned against her for more attention. John walked over to the deer and rabbits, but he kept his eyes on the skunk as it walked near him. Shela asked, "What is up with your hair?" It was sticking out all over the place. Ajh nodded his head, "yeah, I know, who says God does not have a sense of humor. I will put some water on it and straighten it out." Ajh walked to the stream wet his hair and combed it with his fingers.

He walked back, grabbed the bread, handed some to John and Shela and they gave some to the animals, the Ajh gave thanks. "It would be beautiful if the whole world would live like this?" Shela, after taking a bite of bread, said, "Ajh, everyone should know how God wanted it to be." Ajh stared at the ground for a few seconds. "It has been written in the scriptures, many do not read the bible, but those who do, do not understand or cannot see the whole picture the way it was meant to be."

"Most religions teach how to cope with the world as it is, not as it could be. They preach that if we love one another we could have peace and harmony in the world, or they preach how good it is going to feel when we go to Heaven. They should be telling you what you should be doing now to get there, how to be on a righteous path toward God, His way. Religions do not explain in detail the meaning of The Ten Commandments; how strictly we should follow them, and how it could change the world now."

"They separate their religions from each other, and say they are evil. Religions also teach that we are sinners, therefore we can not receive God's power to do miracles like the prophets, but this is a misconception. If religious leaders teach you that you are weak and fall short of the glory of God, then how are you ever going to know the truth, and achieve what Jesus said you can?"

"Some of the prophets were sinners, but they turned to God with absolute faith and belief without doubt. Moses murdered someone, David committed adultery, Solomon did not have to commit adultery with over 700 wives and 300 concubines. But his wives were of other religions and false gods. And Solomon began paying homage to these gods. This made God angry that Solomon did evil and slowly took away what He had given him. This is why we should not jump to marriage, but soften the heart of your future spouse, and follow a path of righteousness toward God. Making sure that your future spouse is right for you and your children to help teach them about God."

"It does not mean we stray away and follow other religions of false beliefs and false gods. We must read the scriptures and the Ten Commandments to understand the true path. So you see, no one is innocent, not even the prophets. But they believed, without doubt, and had faith in God, this is the key that will open doors for you to do miracles, this is what Jesus was trying to teach all of us. Do the will of the Father. Truth comes by understanding. Man does not know the whole truth, God is truth, religions bring confinement and rituals, God sets you free."

"God gave you the Ten Commandments to live by as guidance. If you follow them to the fullest extent, you will find happiness and joy. And there will be harmony for the whole world. Always speak the truth. Everything you do that is good, give God the credit. Say that you do these things in the name of God as Jesus taught you to do. You are children of God; show it in your deeds and actions. Make God proud to call you his child. Love God with all your heart and do his will. That is what God wants, that is what Jesus, Buddha, Mohammed, Moses, and you should want."

John asked, "Ajh, you talk a lot about Jesus. I knew some Jewish people and they thought Jesus was a good prophet, but not the Savior or Messiah. How would you explain it to them?" Ajh paused, "we can all be like Jesus if we listen to his words, though we would not be as pure. But before I answer the question, did they ever tell you what their Messiah was supposed to do for them?" John answered, "I guess take them away from their misery and oppression and into the Promised Land."

Ajh said, "They probably expect their Messiah to give them land, land that belongs to other people. Because there is no more land to claim, it all belongs to someone, which means you would have to kill them or enslave them, and steal the land and all their property. These are all things against God's commandments. If he breaks God's Law, then how can he be the Messiah?"

"Instead the Messiah must come in peace and harmony, and teaching a way of life and love toward God, doing things the right way, God's way, a way of life that is beyond our imagination. Where we become superior beings as God intended. Beings, using God's power to do good, where there are no homes or governments or anything that separates us from each other, to be truly brothers and sisters."

"Tell me, what do you think of God, what kind of person is He? What is His personality, His nature? John replied, "Well, I guess He is all knowing, caring, and truthful, and all seeing." Ajh looked at Shela, "What do you think?" She said, "He is all loving, all forgiving, wants the best for us." Ajh asked, "You mean, if you hated God, He would still love you?" They said, "Yes." "He cares for you even though you do not pay any attention to him."

"If you curse God for all the bad things that happen to you, blaming Him when He is not at fault, but later you realize the wrong you did, and ask God for forgiveness; would not God forgive you and take you under his wing, like a lost child that has come home?" They said, "Yes." "If God was on earth, would he not be preaching a way of life and love that would be different compared to the way the religions preach today?" And He would be preaching about love, kindness, peace and harmony between all people on earth, not just your own kind." They said, "Yes."

"Let's say, because of his words, you hated him, you did not like what he said because it is against your beliefs and what your religion teaches, but he still kept preaching, regardless of all the protests. So a mob came together and beat him until he was dead. Would He not still forgive that mob?" They said, "Yes." "And would He not love everyone equally, whether you are a stranger or a close relative?" They both said, "Yes." Ajh replied, "You have just described Jesus Christ, like Father, like son."

"You see Christ came to show you a way toward the Father. And in following in Jesus' footsteps, you will see the truth and know God. You will understand even deeper, the entity of God and what purpose you have in life to serve Him." Jesus was trying to show you how much love and honor to give the Father and how much love to have toward each other. He died showing you this way of life."

"Take for example Christ's death. Here is a man who loved, showed kindness and compassion to everyone and judged no one. Yet He was betrayed by the people he preached to. Religious leaders questioned Him spit and slapped Him on the face. They took Him to soldiers who punched him in the face until his cheeks and eyes and nose were swollen. Then they whipped him with whips, what the Romans called a flagrum, it had metal or bone dumbbells on the end. It would take out pieces of flesh as they whipped his back. And one soldier even sharpened the metal so it would cut in deeper. They made a crown of thorns that also went on top of His head and punctured it and they laughed, scorn, and spit on him."

"He was brought before Pilot; the people chose a thief and murderer over Jesus to be set free, the very people that he preached to about love and God. He carried his cross through the streets and the people mocked him. When they arrived at the top of the hill, they took his robe off, laid him on the cross, and drove spikes through the base of the hand in the wrist and His feet. Can you imagine a spike being driven through your wrist, splitting the bones, cutting and pinching nerves as it is driven into a board, with each pounding blow? Then your feet and you know how it hurts to injure your instep. Can you imagine a spike going through your feet, what that would feel like?"

"Every time the hammer hits the spike tearing and pinching the nerves, bones, and tendons, as it is driven deeper into the wood, it must have been so much pain. Then the cross is stood up and dropped into a hole. This made the spikes feel like torture. While up on the cross, people were still making fun of him. When He asked for water, they gave him vinegar. And before the blood drained from his body and he died, Jesus looked up to God and said, "*Forgive them Father for they know not what they do.*" If that is not the son of God, then I do not know who is."

There was silence; they were thinking of what Ajh said with tears running down their cheeks. You could hear a gentle breeze rustling through the trees as the sun shined through. It was beginning to be a warm and beautiful sunny day. The animals were quiet, some sitting close together looking at Ajh, as if listening to him.

"Most religions follow the Ten Commandments the best they can. If they would add the teachings of Jesus, people would realize the truth He spoke of, and that He is the Son of God. His teachings would fit into all religions that believe in God the Father. All Jesus asks of you is when you ask God for a blessing, or miracles say you ask God in His name and you will give Him honor."

Shela asked, "So, it is possible for us to do miracles?" Ajh replied, "Have you not been listening to me, Jesus said "*You can do as I have done and even greater than these you can do, if you have faith and belief without doubt*". Now that is the key, belief without doubt and having faith. People may be religious, but they doubt they are worthy to receive power from God, because of their religious teachings. This goes for all people on Earth; everyone can do miracles."

"People do not have faith in God or themselves to carry out God's will. What they do not realize, is that we are all worthy, if we love God and obey His commandments. We must have faith in the words of Jesus and God. People think miracles are just for Jesus, prophets, and chosen people by God, not for them. God is pure energy waiting for everyone to tap in. God wants you to tap in. If you love Him you will tap in."

"Think of God as a tremendous power plant with enough energy for everyone on earth. No one understands how the power can be received or used. Some people receive just a little and rejoice in the joy of God's love, but they still do not realize their full potential. That is like having electricity coming into your house, but have been told if you touch it you will die. So everyone lives by candlelight, no TV, and no household appliances. It seems foolish, all you have to do is learn to respect electricity and look at all the things that we can do with it and it is right there inside your home."

"This is the same with God, He is right there inside your heart. Once you learn to respect God's ways, His laws and you have faith and believe without doubt, you can use his power to do good, there are no limit to what you can do."

"Jesus said, *"When you pray, pray in spirit and do not pray repetitiously as if God does not hear you."* Know in your heart that God heard you and your prayers will be answered. That is why you do not pray repetitiously, because if you pray repetitiously for the same request that means in your heart you are not sure God heard you or will answer your prayers, you only hope he does. Have faith and believe without doubt, and it will be done according to your faith and His will."

"It is odd today when you hear of religions talking about hope; it seems the word hope should not be in a Christian vocabulary. Because if you hope God hears you and answers your prayers, that means you do not have total faith without doubt that He heard you and will answer your prayers. When you take your car to a mechanic and he says I hope it is fixed, how much faith would you have in him? God hears everyone, but only those with complete faith and without doubt, are their prayers answered, faith like the prophets had. Jesus never used the word hope in reference to God."

"Everyone blames God for not doing anything when it is their fault for the problems of the world. Satan has fed these lies to mankind knowing in our stone hearts that we will blame God for our ill will. He is also not testing us as so many religions claim; it is Satan, knowing again we will blame God. But God is watching to see what we are going to do. And God is not going to clean the world of its problems just so we can start all over again. God has interfered before, and mankind still rejected him. He will not interfere unless we ask Him with our hearts and in faith. He no longer punishes mankind; all these problems are our fault, so stand tall in God's ways and know that you have His powers and do something with them."

Shela asked, "But if we expect it, isn't that a little like demanding? Who are we to demand?" Ajh answered, "It is not quite like demanding, a good example is in the prayer, The Our Father. It says, "*Give us this day our daily bread.*" It does not ask God, it says give us. It is not so much demanding as expecting your rightful share of God' power. Do not worry, God knows what is in your heart. He understands your needs, that you ask unselfishly for His power to help others."

Shela asked, "My God, that means it is our fault for all the starving and sick people in the world!?" Ajh answered, "In a way yes, because we disassociate ourselves and the animosity we have toward each other, we do not realize that we can use God's power to help each other. Many people are compassionate, but they feel overwhelmed by the problems of the world and say what can I do? And there are many people that do not think about the lives of others, what others are going through, or how they can help them, they only think of themselves. Follow God; use His power to help people. When those who have fallen away from God see the miracles being done and realize they could do the same, they will realize what they are doing, and begin to change, then they will convert to following God. And do not use God or God's name as an expression, only call on His name to talk to Him or in prayer."

"If you think of yourself last and others first, you will see God. You will know Him and understand Him. Then you can use His power to feed the starving, heal the sick, and even raise the dead. God gave you the freedom to choose, so choose God's path and not man's. Open your eyes to what is going on in the world. Look at everything you do in life, all material possessions and all your achievements, they are all meaningless. It is time to choose God's path. It is time for enlightenment."

Shela asked, "You have the power, why don't you do something about starving people?" Ajh answered, "I have people to teach and things to do for God, to fulfill the scriptures and spread the word. There will be another person that will join me; we will help some starving people, but it is too late because the beginning of the end is at hand."

"We are only experiencing the beginning of sorrows. There will be destruction on earth that mankind has never seen before. The geological structure of this planet is beginning to change. Earthquakes will destroy the cities of the world. Volcanoes will darken the skies. Storms, tornados, floods, and drought will destroy much of the world's food supply along with pestilence, causing famine all over the world."

"A great earthquake will drop California into the ocean. A second quake in Central America will allow the Pacific Ocean to flow into the Atlantic Ocean. The Atlantic coastline will rise; this is in the bible when it says that *"the islands will flee away" and earthquakes in diver's places"*. This will be the cause of destruction of many cities, power plants, and factories. Chemicals and radiation will pollute the air and water, causing breathing problems for all life on earth. The sun will scorch mankind with heat and sores on their skin, and there will be signs that will put fear in people's hearts. There will be a period of suffering and then Judgment Day."

"When Jesus comes, the whole world will know it. Because you will see him in the sky, in the east to the west it will be the same. The whole world will see Him. No one will be able to hide. After the judgment, God will create a new Heaven and Earth. There will be eternal peace and joy, no more suffering, no more tears. *"On earth as it is in Heaven."*

John asked, "What is Judgment Day going to be like?" Ajh answered, "You will be judged by your deeds and how well you obeyed God's laws. You will also judge yourself. God will take out your heart of stone and give you a heart of flesh. Then you will know your sins, your whole life will flash before your eyes, the pain and misery you have caused others, how you have broken God's commandments, and you will not be able to deny the truth. You will know that you do not belong in Heaven."

Shela asked, "Then how can we enter into Heaven? How can we have a chance?" Ajh answered, "Ask God for forgiveness, love thy neighbor, put other people first before yourself, and sin no more. Try with all your heart to follow Christ's footsteps and the Ten Commandments the best you can. If your heart is with God, then you will be with God." Shela and John were quiet. You could hear the birds chirping, the water running through the stream, and a breeze blowing through the tops of the trees."

Shela asked, "Why does God allow mentally challenged people to be born? They can't live a normal life?" Ajh answered, "Well, in the beginning God created Adam and Eve and told them to go and multiply. So it is up to us to reproduce. God gives a soul to an individual in the womb. God lives in everyone. It is up to us to give handicapped people a lot of love and care."

"But instead, they are institutionalized and kept away from society; some say they do not know what they are doing or what is going on around them. But they know they are not receiving love in an institution. There are homes that have given handicapped people love and care and they have astounded doctors on how well the handicapped have progressed. That is all it takes, love, kindness and good care to make a difference in their lives, they are as valuable and worthy as anyone else."

"God created everything perfect, therefore no diseases and no deformities. But as man followed man's path, he created his own problems. Not only in what he ate, but the way he thought also. As for why we have all these different types of deformities? Look at us today we drink and eat chemicals, we breathe in pollution, put chemicals all over our body. Radiation is in the air. They are creating bacteria they can not kill so they release them into the atmosphere. When chemicals mix in our bodies, they disturb the order in which the body functions. Sometimes chemicals are changing the genes, causing an imbalance, not allowing your body to function properly to fight diseases and bacteria."

"It will take science another 20 years to realize how sensitive the body is to chemicals and the damage it can do. But they will not say anything because big business will suffer and they will worry about the economy. Or they will give conflicting reports, so the public will not pay any attention."

"We take medication that is made up of chemicals. Has enough research been done, to find out what will happen to us 10 or 20 years from now? Will it be passed on to our children? Each generation adds to the chemicals in the body and the change in our genes. Just like we pass down our sins from generation to generation, or our ignorance which ever way you want to look at it. It is quite evident in radiation, how people exposed to large doses later on have problems. Developing diseases and passing it on to their children."

"Chemicals, even in small amounts, develop small changes in the genes and the body. If you pollute the world and your bodies, you can not expect God to clean it up, so you can continue polluting, and you can not expect God to eliminate people that do not measure up to society's standards. Mankind created these problems; mankind has to take responsibility for his deeds. If we followed God and believed in His grace nothing would affect us, we would be taken care of."

John asked, "What do you do in Heaven?" Ajh answered, "At first you worship God, thanking him for the joy and peace you have. You might do this for hundreds or thousands of years, just because it feels so good. Then enjoy all the things he created. For example, just think if this world would follow God in spirit. There would be no homes, no countries, no governments, and no borders. You walk the earth and enjoy the beautiful sceneries, sunrises and sunsets. When you have seen it all here, you have the universe to explore."

Shela asked, "What are the children doing in Heaven?" Ajh answered, "right now, play as they always do, enjoying the scenery and beauty of God's creations. John said, "But kids don't care for scenery?" Ajh answered, "oh, but they do. If you do not believe me, ask him." As Ajh looked over their heads an a little up the hill and pointed. They both turned around and looked up the hill and said, "Who is that? Where did he come from?"

There was a young boy with auburn hair, thin build, wearing a white T-shirt, jeans, and sneakers. Ajh said, "Go and follow him, a child can teach you a lot." The young boy waved at them, then waved them on, "come on, follow me, come on!" Ajh said, "go, I will dark out the fire, and send the animals on their way."

So they ran up the hill, following the boy who dotted over too the left and then shot up the hill, through the trees, and kept edging them on "come on, come on!" They were keeping up with him the best they could. The kid was full of energy and very wiry. He scrambled up the hill, like a deer knowing every inch of the path. Finally, Shela and John couldn't keep up with him and take it anymore and yelled "stop!" John breathing heavily, "hold on, let us catch our breath." They were exhausted. Shela asked, "What are we doing anyway," as she was breathing very heavily.

The boy said, "Did you see it, couldn't you feel it all!?" They were still out of breath, "What are you talking about?" The boy answered, "Didn't you see the beautiful, yellow butterfly when you first came up the hill!? John, did you see the markings on the frog sitting on the rock!? Shela, did you feel how soft that moss was that you put your hand on, it was green with red spots, wasn't it pretty!? John, when you grabbed that branch, did you feel how cool the dew was when it fell on your hand!? Or how the wet leaves looked when the sun shined on them!? Didn't you feel the warm sun on your back as you came up the hill!? Did you see that marble stone, white with pretty red markings!? Did you listen to the songs of the early birds!? Or feel the morning cool breeze!?"

Shela and John, still breathing heavily, said "stop!!" Shela asked, "I don't understand all this!?" They both looked down the path with puzzled looks on their faces. Then they both sat down, putting their heads down on their arms, resting on their knees. "I'm confused, I don't understand" John said as he looked up and there was Ajh standing in front of them.

"You can learn much from a child" commented Ajh. Shela looked up, "Where did you come from? Then she looked around "Where did the boy go?" Ajh replied, "He is with God. You do not understand the point, do you?" They both shook their heads. "Think about it, we go through life worrying about the world, and we do not see the beauty of God's creation, and enjoy the things He made within it. Children see this beauty and no one listens to the children. There is a lot you do not pay attention to."

John said, "He couldn't have paid attention to all that!?" Ajh replied, "He uses 100% of his brain, like you are supposed to." Ajh continued up the hill, "come on, you have much more to learn." They started to climb up the hill, only a few feet, and then sat back down. John still out of breath, "Can we sit down and rest a while!?" Shela said, "Yeah, I'm exhausted too!" Ajh replied, "You are not as young as you would like to be?" John remarked, "Well I didn't see you run up the hill!" Ajh answered, "I did not have to." Shela looked up at Ajh. "What do you mean!? How did you get!?" John interrupted, "don't ask, please don't ask!"

Shela started to laugh, then as she caught her breath asked "so the children just play in Heaven?" Ajh sat down next to them on the hillside, "right now yes, but after the judgment things will be different. A new Heaven and earth, Heaven for all that deserve it or hell for those who do not have righteousness in their hearts. As for the children, they will be grown up, and have the maturity of an adult but everyone will have the heart of a child, a heart of flesh."

Shela asked, "What is Heaven like?" Ajh answered, "Heaven can be compared to a beautiful kingdom filled with peace, joy, and serenity. As you walk up, picture in your mind a huge golden gate adorned with pearls and diamonds and the walls decorated with sparkling jewels and precious stones. But before you can enter you must see the man at the gate.

Three men came that wanted to get into the kingdom. The first man walked up and said, "I have much money and power. I can buy you anything you need." The man at the gate said, "We have all we need and you have no power here" and he cast the man into the eternal fire. The second man came and said, "I have lots of land to expand your kingdom, I possess many jewels to adorn its buildings and walls." The man at the gate said, "we have all the room we need for those that are worthy, the jewels are only on the outside of the walls for your purpose, no one possesses anything here, we have no need of earthly jewels" and he cast him into the eternal fire."

"The third man approached the gate. He said, "I am not worthy of such a beautiful place. I have nothing to offer except my heart, soul, and myself as a laborer." The man at the gate smiled and said, "Your heart and soul we will accept, but no one labors here. Please enter and rejoice."

Shela questioned him, "No Ajh that is not what I meant. You gave me an example of what entering into Heaven is like. I mean, what is Heaven really like?" "Well" said Ajh, "that is very difficult to explain if you know nothing of the worlds hereafter." John asked, "What do you mean worlds?" Ajh answered, "That is very difficult to explain, much less to understand. Like I said before there are different levels of Heaven. If we use so many words to explain the world we see, how can you explain or understand the spiritual realm, or dimension as some scientists would say, that you have never experienced before?"

"Tell me this, what would it be like if you did not have a body? Remember, you do not have eyes to see or ears to hear, a nose to smell, or hands to touch. What do you think it would be like?" They both shook their heads and shrugged there shoulders. John said, "It sounds like it would be pretty dull without our senses." Ajh continued, "That is because you only know of this world and what you have experienced with your senses you have here."

Shela asked, "What kind of body do you have?" Ajh answered, "Not a body, a soul or spirit, or you could say an energy form with the personality traits you have now, except being all loving and righteous. This is basically how you identify each other. With God's knowledge and Him living in you, you will know who you are talking to." Shela asked, "Will we be able to see our loved ones?" Ajh answered, "Yes, but you are implying that you are searching for someone you love more than anyone else. In Heaven you will love everyone equally."

"You will have senses but different, you will be able to see, but not as clear as with your eyes. Like seeing through a white veil. Here look at each other through this." As Ajh pulled out from inside his sleeve a small, white, thin veil and handed it to her. She looked through it at John, "yeah, I see what you mean, kind of like looking through a white haze. I don't care for that. I like it nice and clear." Ajh said, "Well you will become use to it and you will not even notice it after a while. And you also will be able to see all around you not just in front of you, remember you do not have physical eyes to see with."

"But look at the advantage of being without a body and with God. Nothing can harm you. You can travel anywhere in the universe with just a thought. Or concentrate yourself to be one with God. And you will be able to see the entire universe and all the details of events at the same time. Watch a volcano erupting in Hawaii while a star explodes in another galaxy, and at the same time, watching the colors of the leaves turning in Maine in the fall, while watching a flower bloom in Brazil."

Shela said, "That's impossible, to see all that at once." Ajh answered, "With man yes, with God anything is possible. There are many things you can do; it is all possible in God's kingdom. If you need your body for any reason, it is always at your disposal to use." She asked, "Why would you need it?" Ajh explained, "Sometimes to do God's work you will need your physical body to communicate with people in the physical world."

"As for the kingdom with buildings and walls that is talked about in the Bible, this will be on earth in a physical form when you want to exist in a physical form. But like I said there is much to explore in the universe if you want too. Come on, we have things to do and a lot to learn" Ajh said as they started climbing to the top of the hill.

As they stood up and followed, Shela put the small veil around her neck, like a scarf. When they reached the top of the hill, they were looking at a flat plain with tall grass that stretched for three miles to a rocky hill where they were heading. The grassland in front of them and the tree line behind them stretched for miles, all the way to the mountains to their right.

It was a beautiful picture, all that green grass, and the gray stone of the rocky hill where they were heading. The hill was peppered with grass, weeds, some small brush and flowers growing here and there all the way up, several hundred feet, but most of the hill was small rocks and ledge. As you looked up you could see how high the hill was, with a clear blue sky in the background. To the right in the distance, you could see the snow on the mountains, but the low clouds surrounding the top, were blocking the view of its peak.

Chapter **VIII**

AJH EXPLAINS ABOUT EVOLUTION AND CREATION

As they started to walk through the tall grass, John asked, "Why are there creatures on earth that resemble each other to give valid point to the evolution theory? I am assuming God created everything?" Ajh explained, "well, how many billions of patents do you think God is going to come up with without having any similarities? Besides, God also has to stay within the genetic makeup of earth." John said, "You mean being carbon based and the same DNA code?" Ajh answered, "Yes. Do you know how many billions of species there are past and present?"

"But think about that for a minute. Why is it written that God created all living things out of the dust of the Earth? If the prophet that wrote that down knew God was all powerful, would he not say God created everything out of thin air. Knowledge had to be given to him to use the word dust so there would be a carbon base relation, and God is the source of all knowledge."

"Let us start from the beginning with the big bang. First of all, scientists do not believe in God, who always was and always will be. But they believe in a rock that was an eventually will be, or did the rock just appear. Some new theories say that all the matter was compact in an atom or black hole. Then where did the matter come from and what made it explode and why is it that black holes do not explode today?"

"Let us look at the big bang itself. The explosion is supposed to have spread matter throughout the universe. If you look at the example of a shotgun being fired, the BB's when they first come out of the barrel, start separating immediately and will continue to separate as long as there is a force behind the BB's. So if whole galaxies are being pushed away from each other today from the big bang, then how could two small dust particles 13 billion years ago(according to evolution) when the force was stronger, pull themselves together to start forming planets and stars, when a stronger force was separating them?"

Ajh paused, "now here are some confusing thoughts. The word black hole sort of contradicts itself. A hole is an empty space or a tear in space, like a worm hole. But a black hole that scientists are talking about is a collapsed star or solid matter. It should be called a (black star), producing energy and light we cannot see."

"Scientists also found dark energy and dark matter. Dark energy provides gravity and motion to keep galaxies for the most part in their place. Of course, there are exceptions to the rule when you see colliding galaxies. Now dark matter, they say, is just floating out there. Now would not black holes or (black stars) pull in all the dark matter after billions of years, there would not be anything left because the (black star) should be getting larger and in time eliminate what is floating out there."

"Then you have some scientists that waste their time contemplating time travel. Which ever you believe in, God, or the universe, neither would allow it. The damage you could do by upsetting the time line, think of all the scenarios of going back in time, bringing back bacteria from the future into the past that wipes out mankind. Then if mankind does not exist, then he cannot use time travel and does that mean that man reappears again? It is stupidity. I think they have been watching too much science fiction and look at all the time and tax dollars they waste contemplating and experimenting such nonsense, something they could never prove. If you go back in time and see someone that is dead, how is that possible, are you visiting the spirit world which science does not believe in?"

"You can view the past, but you cannot participate in it." John asked, "What do you mean, view the past?" Ajh answered, "Well you know that if you travel far enough out into space, you can pick up the first television program ever broadcasted. Because it is still traveling outward. Well, if they had the technology, they could pick up somewhere out in space the events of the past. You see, everything is made up of atoms and energy that vibrate at a certain frequency. Scientists have been able to record sounds the planets and stars make. The stars, moons, planets, and people, and events of what is going on, vibrate and are traveling outward. Now if man had the technology, and was able to travel deep enough into space to pick up these frequencies, he would be able to view the past."

"They have not found worm holes as of yet. Some scientists believe that a black hole or (black star) and a worm hole are the same. That is foolish, whereas a (black star) generates energy and light we can not see, and a large amount of gravitational pull and is made up of condensed matter. A worm hole, on the other hand, is an opening between two points in space, like a tear in space itself. To create a worm hole you need two opposing forces, either gravitational or electromagnetic to tear space apart, to create an opening. Then you would need an event somewhere else in space, opening the other end of the worm hole with the same frequency. And a wormhole does not take you to another point in time. It is not a time portal."

John and Shela said, "whoa, whoa. You are getting way over our heads! Let's get back to evolution!" Ajh said, "I'm sorry, I am getting carried away again." He continued as they walked through the field of grass. "But may I add that, all these theories scientist come up with are built on a theory from another theory with other theories. If the equations are all theoretical how can they prove what they are saying? Is there any solid evidence?"

"Now let me point out that evolution and creation the way it is stipulated in the bible, have a lot of similarities. For example, in Genesis in the beginning it says *"the earth was without form, and void and darkness was upon the face of the deep. And the Spirit of God moved upon the face of the waters. And God said, Let there be light. And God saw the light, that it was good. And God divided the light from the darkness."*

"Now let us look at this one step at a time. The earth was without form and void in darkness. Does not science believe that the earth was formed before the sun? If the sun was not formed yet, what would keep the planets in orbit without the gravity of the sun? And would not the sun pull in the matter from Earth to form itself?"

"The light God was talking about was His light, because the sun, moon, and stars were not made yet. And to divide the light from the darkness and using the word void were odd words to use. The only place you can divide light from darkness and be void is in space. The earth was without form. This is the matter God created and brought it together to form earth. And God called this "the first day." Now a day of God is the universe and the galaxies revolving around Him, so a day for Him could be billions of years to us." To God and the spiritual world time means nothing."

"On the second day God created the firmament and on the third day he made the dry land appear. Now the word here is land not with an S at the end, meaning one land mass as scientist believes it was in the beginning. He created the seas, made the grass, and the herbs, and the fruit trees. On the fourth day, God created two lights, the greater light to rule the day, which is the sun and the lesser light (the moon) to rule the night, and he made the stars. So a day up to this point were God's days, or as a reference all seven days of creation would be according to His time, because it was not until the fourth day that the sun was made. So it was God's light that flourished on earth to make the plant life grow, which is why He saw the light was good, because only God is good."

Shela asked, "Then why do we see stars and galaxies being formed today, if God created them all billions of years ago?" Ajh answered, "He did not create them all in the beginning. He is creative and is still creating today. The universe is expanding so there is always room for more stars and galaxies. Do scientist have an explanation for where all this gas comes from to form stars and galaxies? No they do not; their only explanation is the Big Bang. Wait till they start exploring the universe they will be surprised at how ignorantly they think today. If they ever make it out into space past our solar system."

"Back to creation, then God created life in the water, all the creatures and foul, after their kind, and it was the fifth day. He created the cattle and creepy things, and beasts on earth. And may I add that each pause was millions of years to us. Because how could creatures go and multiply in one day?"

"Then God made man in his image, that is to say man would have God's spirit in him. And God made woman from man's rib and this was done on the sixth day; remember we are still using God's days. Because Adam was on the Earth for a while; naming all the animals and taking care of the Garden of Eden. God made the garden and put Adam there to tend to it. Then God said that Adam needed help so He created woman."

"Now God made man and all the creatures out of the ground. That would show why we are all carbon-based and have the same basic genetic code. Most of this is the same order as science calls evolution, except the part of plant life starting before the sun was completely formed. Now, how could a prophet know all this, and most of all, that man was the last being to come about? If man thought so much of himself, would he not put himself as being created first?"

"Science also believes today that the atmosphere was not developed in the beginning to have clouds and to rain, but a low fog would water the plants. In the bible, in Genesis, Chapter 2:5-6, it says that *"God had not caused it to rain upon the earth in those days and there was no man to till the ground, but a mist from the earth went up and watered the whole face of the ground."* If science only discovered this about fifteen years ago, how could a prophet have written it down thousands of years ago about something that happened long before man existed."

"Does science really have a good explanation where all the water came from to fill the oceans? And all the snow an ice in the North and South Pole combined would cover the Earth. To explain how God created the universe, a good example is the formula E=MC², which is energy, equals matter times the speed of light squared. The formula is not totally accurate, because you do not need the speed of light squared to create energy and the speed of light is not constant. But the formula is close enough. By rearranging the formula you can find out how God created the universe."

"For example, in electronics to find the volts in a circuit, you use the formula, E=IxR, volts equals amperage time's resistance or (ohms). So if you want to find resistance, you would change the formula to R=E/I. So in God's case, to find matter, you already have God, which is pure unlimited energy and light, with the speed of thought, so the formula is M=E+C^t. That is matter equals energy plus light at the speed of thought. Thus the creation of the universe."

"Everything is made up of energy. Scientists today, using a cyclotron, can bombard metal with electrons; as a result they can change a metal to have the same qualities as gold. God with unlimited energy can create and change matter. Jesus fed thousands of people with a few fish and bread. He used God's energy to do this. Even Satan, knew that Jesus could change stone to bread when he tempted him. So you see, anything is possible if you have the right knowledge to achieve what you want."

"To those who think the universe, earth and all living things, were only created in the seven days of man, and only about 6000 years ago or 4,000 B.C., it is because they believe in religious leaders who do not seek the truth and they follow the path of those who refuse to think. Remember when religions taught that the earth was the center of our solar system and galaxy. That the sun revolved around the earth, and if you believed otherwise, you would be expelled from the church. We are on the outskirts of our galaxy with over two hundred billion stars, and there are billions and billions of galaxies, (as Ajh changed his voice and they laughed). So why judge a day of God by our small point of view?"

"To prove that the earth has been here for hundreds of millions, even billions of years all you would have to do is go outside at night where there are no city lights and look at the stars, a higher elevation would be better. Some of those stars are not stars at all, but whole galaxies billions of light years away. Now light travels at 186,000 miles per second for the most part. A light year is light traveling at that speed for a full year. The light you see from these stars and galaxies took millions, even billions of years to travel to earth for you to see them. So if the Earth was only here since around 4,000 B.C., according to people who interpret the Bible by following the genealogy of the descendants of the prophets, you would only be able to see less than .01% of all those stars in the sky. Seek the truth as your Heavenly Father wants you too."

"For those who follow the genealogy of the descendents in the Bible, Do they not think it is odd that there are 50 chapters in Genesis that cover about 2500 years, yet only 7 chapters cover the creation of the universe, earth, the multiplying of all living things on earth, the dinosaurs and their extinction, including man populating the whole Earth, man's fall away from God, the destruction of man to Noah and the flood? Then populating the Earth again. And much of what is said is repeated in the 7 chapters. There is also very little information about how the three sons of Noah, or Cain as he was cast off, could go and multiply and covered the Earth. How one son would go and start a new nation, city or country. When some of his sons would live a hundred years before having a son. And that is something to think about why man went a hundred years before having another child, or a son, you mean he did not touch his wife for a hundred years?"

"Then there were giants before the flood and after the flood, when all living things on the earth perished in the flood. Also God reduced the age of man to 120 years, and still man continued to live 400 or more years afterwards. Some to 900 years that stood on a path with God. I believe there is a lot of information that is missing. Archeologists have to find more scriptures to fill in the missing years and genealogy of other descendants of man. They should look around the world because man has carried information with him in his travels and the Earth has changed a lot since then."

Ajh paused for a few moments, "now back to evolution and the Bible. God said, "*I give you all green herbs and fruits from the trees for meat.*" That means we were meant to be vegetarians and we are like vegetarian animals. We have flat molars and the enzymes in our stomach with a long stomach lining, which are all the same characteristics of a vegetarian animal. According to science, man has been eating meat for millions and millions of years. If we evolve like they claim, that means our systems would change to adapt to what we are eating without harm."

Shela asked, "What harm does it do to our bodies?" Ajh answered, "Well if you look at all the countries that were poor and vegetarian, then as the country prospered and began eating meat, cancer and other diseases were on the rise. Pollutants and chemicals in the air and water are a factor also."

"But eating meat with a long stomach lining causes the meat to go rancid in your stomach. All animals that eat meat have a short stomach lining, so that it will digest and quickly pass through. Plus the chemicals they have in the meat we eat, and in the blood, that causes diseases. And have you noticed that doctors are telling people to stay away from red meat and eat more fruits and vegetables for better health? As much as they are suggesting you to eat you would be too full to eat any meat."

John asked, "I thought God gave the okay to eat meat?" Ajh continued, "Not in the beginning when He created mankind. Then when mankind insisted on eating meat, God told him what meats he could eat and to drain the blood. We eat all kinds of meat and do not drain the blood."

"Now, let us get back to evolution. In the beginning according to science which says all living things started from a one cell amoeba, a very simple life form. The one cell became two cells, then four, eight, sixteen, and so on until it became a life form similar to a jellyfish. According to science, each change in a life form occurs because of a need from the environment or whatever. But if a one cell amoeba is surviving just the way it is, then what is the reason for it to change into a two cell amoeba, and you would have to ask yourself that question for every change for billions of cells until it becomes a jellyfish."

"Then you would have to ask yourself what is the reason for it to change again and having a vertebra, bones, lungs, fins, stomach intestines, and eyes. How does a fish know it needs eyes, when it does not know what they are? If the odds of a life form ever existing are a billion to one, you would have to give those odds to each change, from a one cell amoeba all the way to man. And if the system is perfect the way it is, what is the reason to change. Look how complex our system is and all the creatures on earth. The odds are, by evolutionary standards, not very good of life evolving the way they said."

"In evolution, each species kept changing into a better one. Yet scientists have found bones of dinosaurs, sea creatures and insects that have not changed for millions of years. Why does evolution stand still for some and march on for others? Bees have not changed in millions of years. And royal jelly turns an ordinary bee into a queen bee. How can all this happen without divine intervention in the design of the DNA? Some of the species of dinosaurs and animals came about from cross breeding two different species. In the beginning, God said to *"go and multiple after their kind."* But on occasion they would mingle and crossbreed."

"Evolution does not explain why two birds living in the same environment and eating the same food are different in size, color, and beak size and their habits are different. God gave all creatures the capability to adapt to their environment and change for their protection. But adapting does not mean creating a new creature except in the case of crossbreeding."

"You know that if you breed a horse and ass together you get a mule. Think of a scenario that if the world was destroyed and we resort back to farming and after 10,000 years science starts believing in evolution again. If they found the bones of a mule, horse and ass, they would think the mule came first, and the horse and ass separated on the evolutionary scale from that point? You see if you do not have all the information, how can you come to a conclusion? Science is willing to pick apart the Bible, and those who believe in it to find flaws to justify its claims about how ignorant religious people are. But no one picks apart evolution with all its flaws, especially in genetics. Or point out the terrible things atheists are doing without any moral background. If you are taught that you came from an animal then it is easy to act like an animal. You should not look at the ignorance of others because of their beliefs, but because of their lack of knowledge. We are all ignorant of the truth."

"In the beginning, even people were able to marry brother and sister, nephew and aunt, and so on and they were intelligent people with no abnormalities. Hitler experimented with interbreeding and he created some geniuses and a lot of mentally challenged people. And I have heard of a cat and rabbit interbreeding on a farm. One is a predator and one is a prey, how does evolution explain that?"

"Science also says our diseases and physical problems are hereditary, that they are passed down through the genes. If that were totally true, mankind would be extinct by now. Each generation would be weaker, with no cures thousands of years ago people would no longer exist.

Remember we follow the same pattern as our parents, eating the same foods, having the same habits and living in the same area. And our problems multiplied when people started believing that everything is hereditary."

"Let us get back to evolution and man. If we came from an ape, where did the ape come from? How come they have no bones of creatures being the ancestor of ape? Why does the ape still exist? All creatures on earth, their ancestors are dead, yet the ape still exists."

"And all others between ape and man have become extinct, why? If we came from an ape, then we are the weaker of the two. How does this fit in with survival of the fittest? Being weaker, we would have been subjected to predators and the ape would have to care for us more."

"Look at all the differences between man and ape. In activity and development, it takes man almost twice as long to focus eyes, crawl, sit up, stand erect, walk, and sexually mature. If we are advanced, why does it take us longer? How could our bodies change so we even live twice as long, when prehistoric creatures lived longer then the generations later on?"

"Now let us look at the bone structures. The legs, arms, rib cage, hands, feet, and teeth are all different. On man the shoulder blades are smaller and positioned differently, and the neck bones are smaller. The skull on an ape has a crown and a lobed forehead with larger eye sockets and is thicker. What would be the reason for all these changes if all we needed were different hips to walk upright, a larger brain, and opposable thumbs?"

"And if all these changes are gradual, then where are all the bones of these creatures with the gradual changes? They only found a few skulls that are a little different, but not all the bone changes they talk about. And they are not really sure if they are human bones. Are they normal or could they be a mutation from living near radioactive material? Has any scientist considered that? Where they have found large grave sights of dinosaurs, not to far off there are radioactive mines."

"The brain size of an ape is about a third of man, yet the ape brain usage potential is only approximately 26%. While man has a potential of 100%, more so if that person is with God. The reason we do not use full potential is because of our beliefs in man's way of thinking, superstitions, and the way we are educated."

"Although science may say we are using 100% but not all at the same time. If we did then everyone would have ESP, photographic memory, speed reading, and the list is endless. Another thing about the brain, there are humans with a disease that causes the brain to be smaller than the ape. Yet their intelligence is normal for humans, which contradicts the belief that the size of the brain determines the intelligence of the individual."

"Remember this, the difference between a genius and a layman is that a genius chooses to use more of his mind, where as a layman accepts what level he is in and does not expand his mind any further. When science compares an ape and man, they tone down the ape and show a muscular man. Man is not normally muscular; unless he over-exercises a lot, which he would not do back then."

"Years ago they always showed dinosaurs with gray and green skin. Today they have colors with all different shades and spots, why, so the public will accept it better, or maybe it will fit into their theory better to explain the markings on today's animals. Why are all the animals' different colors? If it is for camouflage, then why are not all ground animals in the same area or all tree animals have the same color? As for dinosaurs, how do they know the color or how much hair, if all they have are bones? They only have a few skin samples with no color."

Shela asked, "Why did God create creatures that look like man?" Ajh answered, "Actually they look like ape. Science always claims they are man's ancestors, but they are more like apes' cousins. God made many creatures like ape and monkey and a few somewhat like man. But they are animals, no higher intelligence, morals, ideals, and no connection to God."

"Science is a little mixed up in their theories. For example Cro-Magnon man, with new evidence seems to have appeared on four continents at the same time. All the changes were also at the same time, brain enlargement, vocal track for speech, smaller brow, thin skull wall for larger brain, pointer chin. There is no evidence of a gradual change all changes were spontaneous. Now according to evolution, if we change because of our environment, then how could we change on four different continents at the same time?"

"And may I add there have been several Ice Ages, caused by eruptions, by what they are calling now super volcanoes. When an Ice Age comes and wipes out many life forms, does evolution start all over again creating new creatures to fit the environment, and how does it happen so quickly?"

"They also have evidence that man was mining 15,000 years ago and grinding tools 160,000 years ago. He cultivated crops and domesticated animals before the last glacial period. They have evidence of cultivated corn dating back 80,000 years ago in Mexico, long before it was believed man existed on the American Continents. From Canada to South America there is evidence that we have been here for a long time."

"They found pottery dating back 50 million years, which predates (by 25 million years) when ape and man separated on the evolutionary tree. They also have some artifacts, for example, three stone balls with rings or ridges that are perfect in shape and they date back 150 million years. This is if their dating process is accurate. There are footprints in Texas of man and dinosaur walking side by side. It was long thought that someone carved man's footprints on the side of the dinosaurs, as a hoax. But archeologists followed the footprints to some stone slabs. When they lifted the slabs, there were the footprints side by side, man and dinosaur, so man has been here a lot longer and it also shows that he domesticated the dinosaur."

"They also found evidence of Cro-Magnon man, that he practiced religion much earlier and started a search for a spiritual contact on four continents at the same time. They had religious ceremonies in caves, believed to be a downward path into the spiritual world, and it was called a shaman type practice. Saying the word shaman practice and a downward path into the spirit world indicates more of a practice of religion away from God. This would come at a time when mankind lost the word of God and looked for other spiritual feelings and he became lost. This practice of entering deep into the cave to seek spiritual enlightenment is still practiced in many cultures around the world."

"There is a religion in the east, a different order of Buddhist monks, where when one becomes a lama priest, he must go down deep into the caves in the mountains, several hundred feet down. In these caves there are rooms where he must fast and meditate for days. In the rooms there are drawings and writings on the walls of a time long ago when man and woman were giants. The earth also was different, the day shorter and warmer. Tibet was close to the ocean, the earth revolved in the opposite direction. Then the earth was struck by an asteroid causing extinction of the dinosaur. (According to, The Third eye, author T. Lobsang Rampa)."

"The asteriod also slowed down the rotation and changed the direction it is today, and the Earth became cooler. The asteroid was not the only reason for the extinction of the dinosaurs. But whether these stories about these cave drawings are true or not, no one will ever know because they are protected by religious groups and tribes all around the world. The question is, if science was to find some of these caves with evidence that goes against the evolutionary theory, would they come forward and show the world or would they hide this information until they can come up with a plausible explanation to discredit them?"

"Science already has information on the latest discoveries about the genes. That it would take much longer for the genes to change from ape to man, than the time span they think the two became separated on the evolutionary tree, in other words, millions of years longer."

"According to the new studies of biology, of the study of sea to land creatures, it would take 50,000 changes in the genes for a creature to change to go from sea to land. Why do scientists hide this information, because it contradicts their theories or are they scared that people will start thinking on their own? If a scientist tells the public of these findings, they are black balled from the scientific community. Is this what they call science? They are supposed to be searching for the truth. Darwin was ignorant of biology's complexity. Darwin said that if the gradual changes in the bone structure of animals were not found then his theory would not hold up? It has been more than 120 years of digging and no gradual changes have been found. Then why does science still believe in evolution?"

"Darwin also studied birds on an island and found different species because of the size and shape of the bird and the size and shape of the beak. Now through new studies scientist have found that the birds have changed back to the size they were before and that this happens periodically because of climate and food sauce and supply. This is also what happens to humans. Depending on the climate and type of food and abundance would depend on how tall, or weight size and where they are located would also determine the color. Look at here in America with the abundant of food supply most are over weight, but the height varies. A lot of their theories claim people were shorter thousands of years ago, which they have proven wrong. And if we were shorter millions of years ago then how could we come from an ape, when if an ape stands upright he is taller than most people today."

"Here are a few unexplained questions about nature and evolution. There is a dung beetle that collects three chemicals from animal dung. Separate these three chemicals and they are harmless, but if you put them together they will explode. The beetle keeps these three chemicals in three separate chambers. Now according to evolution, how could the very first beetle know enough to keep these chemicals separated? If the very first beetle had mixed the chemicals, it would have exploded and that would have been the end of that species, or the beetle would have been discouraged from trying it again. There is only one answer; God gave the beetle its genetic code to know enough to keep the chemicals separated."

"In evolution you would have to ask yourself, how on the billions of creatures on earth, and the billions of changes in the genes, when you look at the very first one of each species. Even the butterfly, how did the very first caterpillar know enough to spin a cocoon, so it would change into a butterfly?"

"I remember reading about a photographer who took pictures around the world of butterflies and moths. He found and photographed on their wings the English alphabet and the numbers zero through nine. How does evolution explain that? God knows, that at a time when mankind is capable of traveling around the world and studying such things, that this would give him food for thought, that everything came about by intelligent design."

"There is also a carnivorous plant in South America that gives off a rotting meat odor to draw in small rodents and insects to feed on. Now, how does a plant know enough to develop a rotting meat odor, let alone, how does it know what it is? According to evolution, this is impossible unless they are going to tell everyone that plants can think."

"Another thing that is curious, science used to say that oil comes from dinosaurs. If that were true, did all the dinosaurs go to one place to die and then be buried? Because if they lay dead on the ground, the meat would have been eaten by other predators, insects, and birds? Or it would have dried up and rotted. And if they were buried, it would take an awful lot of dirt to fall on them in one spot to bury them as deep as what oil companies are drilling for around the world today, looking for oil. Then ask yourself, how many dinosaurs does it take to make a barrel of oil? Look how many barrels we have used in the last hundred years, and how much is still in the ground, it does not make sense does it? Actually, oil comes mostly from algae."

All this time, while Ajh was talking, they were walking across the large field of grass. You can see that the grass went all the way to the bottom of the rocky hillside, where they were heading. They still had about a mile to go. It was a warm, clear day. The sun was beating on them with a nice breeze coming across the field; the tall grass was wavering in the wind.

Ajh continued, "Here is something interesting, Yogis have been meditating and doing breathing exercises for hundreds of years. Yogis say there is prana energy in the air we breathe to help our bodies and muscles stay in good health. If you would have asked a scientist 60 years ago about prana energy, he would tell you it is some religious nonsense, but today we know there are positive and negative ions in the air we breathe for good health. Only today, we are breathing mostly bad air. The only place for good air is deep in the woods or near the ocean."

"If you had asked scientists 100 years ago about sub-atomic particles so small they travel right through you, the earth, and keep on going, he would tell you it is science fiction nonsense, but now we know it is true. Science just needs time to study the complexity of the universe and how God created it."

"On the internet they have pictures of dragons and giants that they found, more than likely they are fakes, or it would have been publicized by the news media. People publish these lies to see if they can be famous because of myths and legends from different cultures, that have been passed down and people believe in them. If they were true science would discredit the findings or keep it silent because they have no explanation. But you can find the truth in the bible, it says, *"There were giants in those days."* Nobody knows how big these giants were."

"According to the Bible when David slew Goliath, that giant was supposed to be six cubits and a span tall. A cubic is 18 to 22 inches long and a span is about 9 inches. That would make him 9 feet 9 inches to a little lest than 12 feet tall. This giant wore a helmet made of brass, the coat he wore weighed 5000 shekels, a shekel is like a coin the size of a nickel to a quarter. He had greaves of brass on his legs and a target of brass between his shoulders. His spear staff was like a weaver's beam, the spear head weight was 6 hundred shekels of iron. I would say to carry this much weight and to do battle, he would have to be closer to, if not more than 12 feet tall."

Ajh paused a little and continued, "You know, science does not believe in the supernatural because it does not follow the known laws of nature and physics. But the fact is science just has not discovered the laws of the spiritual world. In the dictionary supernatural means "an order of existence beyond the natural world pertaining to a divine power." But in the movies and on TV, most come across as anything supernatural has to do with demons and evil spirits of all kinds."

"Also science does not believe in the spirit world, or life after death, yet they believe in multiuniverses. That is the same as other dimensions, or the spirit world is it not? Because they do not believe in life after death, they made up a theory where there are parallel universes so that when they die here on this Earth their identity and name lives on in a parallel universe. Talk about science fiction and self egos. There is no such thing as a parallel universe where you live out a different scenario of your life. Can you imagine spending your life contemplating how the universe began, multiple universes, time travel or where is all the matter in the universe? They will never in their life time find the answer, instead of believing in God and just enjoy it. " Ajh paused, "Now where was I, I was making a point?

Shela asked, shaking her head, "Do you have ADD or something?" Ajh answered laughing, "Yeah I do why?" Shela answered "because you change subjects a lot and forget what you where talking about." They all laughed. Ajh said, "I know, I never knew I had it until all this talk of ADD came out and I looked into it. When I was in High School my electronics teacher pulled me to the side and said, "You are looking at me as if you are paying attention, but your mind is in another world." I thought it was a bad habit I had. Nobody knew anything about ADD back then, so there was no way of correcting it. Now where was I?" Shela answered, "You were talking about what is on TV and in the movies and the supernatural."

Ajh continued, "Oh yeah, well Hollywood also shows people that are into the Bible becoming mass murders, or part of a cult. This is Satan's way of influencing the people in Hollywood and steering the public away from the spirit world. The movie industry knows how to scare people creating all kinds of demons. But if they saw what Satan's creatures really looked like, Hollywood's creatures are laughable. And they show the good guy killing the bad guys, and acting not much differently."

"They also do not have a clue what an angel is really like. Even the actors and actresses are helping Satan by accepting these roles thinking there is nothing wrong with it, but they are helping to get Satan's message across with sex and violence added. They also use phrases from the Bible too lure you into their way of thinking. If you are helping Satan, then you are against God and all that He stands for."

"Where as, those who have a supernatural experience with God, they know the beauty and purity of God's world. Soon, there will be a sign from God that everyone will see, and it will be able to be photographed and televised, and the whole world will see it. Science will try to come up with an answer, but none the majority will accept and the public will finally realize they have been lied to and led astray. It will be the Dark Ages all over again."

"The newspapers, magazines, TV, radio, and movies are all very good at demeaning God, especially since most of the reporters, editors and writers have been brainwashed in college that evolution exists and God does not. With most people, it starts in grade school. Kids are taught by their teachers, that evolution is the way we came about. They use the word evolved, even in children's programs. The kids cannot talk about God or even say "God Bless You" in the classroom. No one stands up for God. Not to mention the fact that what the teachers are doing is illegal because Congress passed that bible study can be done in school as long as it is student run. Parents should push for changes against these teachers and school departments that try to stop God from being in the classrooms. It is their constitutional right."

"These people are atheist and insist on others believing in their religion. You know it is odd, when you think about it, scientists that believe in evolution and think we are ignorant for believing in creation, yet they look up to Einstein as the father of all their research. Einstein believed in God and was trying to figure out how God made the universe and what God was doing with sub-atomic particles. Maybe that is why Einstein was so smart! God gave him the answers! *Ask and you shall receive.*"

"And did not Einstein say "Religion without science is blind, science without religion is lame." He was right, but I think he meant, science without God is lame. If science and religion do not embrace each other, you will see that history will repeat itself. The Dark Ages will come again. People will burn science books when they learn the truth. And that also goes for religion; they cannot hide behind ignorance for ever. Religion should use science to explain how God created everything, to marvel at His creativity. If you ask God He will give you the answers you are looking for."

"There is no direct evidence that evolution exists, that is why they call evolution a theory. Species do adapt and they do crossbreed. And every 10 to 20 years science changes their theories because they find new information that does not fit their old theories. Here is another thing, why do they insist on studying the monkey when there are other animals more intelligent than the ape. The dolphin and I think there is a species of whale that is more intelligent than an ape. The rat seems to have complex form of thought, which means being able to contemplate what it knows, this was normally thought of as a human or primate trait. Now they have found the raven might be more intelligent than the ape, so it seems our so-called ancestor is sliding down on the intelligence scale. And a frog's bone structure is close to humans."

"Because science claims we came from an animal, most people act like an animal with no fear of God's punishment. They are not giving any thought to the consequences of their action. The beast, or Satan, is influencing society as much as he can. Through the centuries Satan confused people with the interpretation and meaning of God's words. Even to the point of killing each other in the name of religion, God, or freedom, when God said, "*Thou shall not kill.*"

"Then in the last hundred years, it was Satan's last chance to win over as many people as he could, we had two world wars, a century of conflict, even killing people that strive for peace. Evolution convinced many people we were animals and God does not exist. Satan promoted sexuality as a way of life, do it if it feels good. What harm will there be if you are not hurting anyone? Look out for number one, have an attitude. Disrespect your parents. Steal from work or the government, the list is endless."

"Satan has been here for a long time bringing out the greed, selfishness and ignorance to make it easy to stray away from God." John asked, "Is his name 666, what does that mean? Ajh answered, "As I said before He can come in many forms. Satan has come out of the politics of man, to make men gather to worship the beast and follow him, to organize men of greed. The name he has taken is easy to decipher, there are six letters in each of his three names."

"Now, back to evolution, if we are animals, and animals have meaningless sex and homosexuality, then it must be okay. But are we not supposed to be more intelligent that an animal, to have guide lines and morals? Without God, Heaven and hell, then there is no punishment for how immoral we act. Some people even have sex with animals and post it on the internet, like they have no shame at all, when God said to stone them to death. Now we have VD, AIDS, and other diseases that came from animals and people having sex with them."

"In the movies and on TV they keep programming immoral ideas and behavior. You do not realize it but your mind is being programmed with free sex, human sex slaves, cheating on your spouse, homosexuality, murder, torturing of humans and more. Even in sports, which show people beating on each other, is this righteous in God's eyes? And parents think it is ok for their kids to be watching this beating on another human for entertainment. They can not see what their children will be like in the future. All this sounds a lot like the Roman coliseums, does it not? They were pagans with a thirst for sex and blood, and they were a powerful nation, but Rome did fall and history will repeat itself."

"The kids today are raised up with all this sex and violence on TV and even in their video games, not to mention the billboards with subliminal advertisements of sex, death, and homosexuality. Everyday these billboards are programming their minds and each generation becomes desensitized to the feelings of others and with immoral behavior. If a child is brought up with cartoons with half naked girls, G rated movies with sexual implications, and using the word evolved to explain where everything came from, how will they ever have moral and spiritual guidance toward God? As a society we need to wake up and realize what we are doing and what is going on around us."

"Even in the music of today and on the videos, it is all about sex and violence, if kids look up to these people and the music and movie stars entice the kids to join them in their lewd dancing and the way they dress and act. How can they know right from wrong? Yet the parents think it is harmless. Like they say in the bible, each generation passing their sins down to the next generation until they are so far away from God they cannot see the light. They will suffer for their inequities and the way they blasphemy God's name, only those that are pure will be taken to Heaven spiritually."

Shela asked, "You mentioned homosexuality, are you saying it is wrong?" Ajh answered, "It is not of God. Sodom and Gomorrah were destroyed because of their immoral acts of free sex and with anyone. God created man and woman, but that does not mean it is okay for a heterosexual to have meaningless sex. God created man and woman to love each other and to have children. No one has the right to judge homosexuals; it is only God's place to judge. And people should not hate homosexuals or be violent towards them; this is not the way of God. *"Love thy neighbor as thy self"* no matter who or what they are."
"Actually, everyone should abstain from sex and with meditation and fasting, you will be so close to God, you will become a god on earth doing the will of the Father. God said, *"Ye are all Gods;"* that is your

destiny. By following Jesus' footsteps you will find your rightful place, *"on earth as it is in heaven."*

"As for homosexuality, most of them are not homosexuals at all. They are addicted to the fluids and act of sex. As long as they can have sex anytime they want and with anyone, they make up excuses or convince themselves it is okay. It starts off as a curiosity to know what it is like, and because it arouses them they continue, then it becomes a psychological condition as well as a physical one, and because society is accepting it, then they are willing to admit they are homosexuals."

"The psychological part is evident in many of the wrong behaviors, even murdering, stealing, and cheating on your spouse, and so on. The first time, there is a spark in the subconscious telling you it is wrong, that is the spark of God that is there in your heart and soul, but as you convince yourself that it is okay and you try it and it excites you, you keep doing it. Just like stealing, the adrenalin of the possibility of getting caught excites you, so you want to do it again. You make up excuses, like the insurance companies will reimburse them and you need the money, then you convince yourself it is okay. The same with murder, prostitution, homosexuality, and whatever else is not of God."

"As for homosexuality, only about 3% of the nation are homosexuals, yet they are trying to force the rest of the nation to accept it on TV, in the movies, and it is thrown in your face whether you like it or not. Every show has some homosexuality in it. Some of the commercials have subliminal homosexual messages, it programs the mind so you will accept it, and your children are watching all this."

"As for people being born feeling like they belong to the opposite sex, or they have partial organs of both sexes, God knows and understands what they are going through as long as they do not join society and have sex with anyone and everyone they meet. The reason for the two organs is, again the chemicals we put in our bodies from generation to generation."

"And because society accepts homosexuality, science is not looking for a cause or a cure, especially when it is from the chemicals altering our genes. No one wants to say anything against the big corporations because they will lose money and everyone worries about the economy. Besides, the big corporations might come out with contradicting reports, so no one will pay any attention to the original research."

"Some people turn to homosexuality only because they feel uncomfortable with the opposite sex. And more comfortable being around people of the same sex, but that does not mean you have sex with them. There is someone out there that is perfect for you of the opposite sex you just have to find them. Ask God for help and take your time looking for the right person."

"In the Bible, Jesus mentions there are eunuchs who were born that way from their mother's womb and eunuchs who were made eunuchs by men, and there are eunuchs who made themselves eunuchs for the sake of the Kingdom of Heaven. The word eunuchs means, being castrated or not being able to have sex. And there are those who refrain from sex for the sake of God, they will be close to him and have a special place in Heaven."

"So if people find themselves in this situation, think of God and what he has to offer. They should ask God to guide them on the right path, He will answer. Have faith in Him. You also have to remember that homosexuality is not the only outcome of chemicals altering the genes. There is autism, cancer, ADD, diabetes, and many other problems that are increasing in our society. ADD is also caused partially by TV and other such devices that act on the mind or keeping the mind blank while feeding all this nonsense people watch. More directly affecting children when they are young. All these problems are caused by man's so-called advancements, if that is what you want to call it. The problems of today will continue to get worse until the destruction of all things. Then God will remove everything he did not create, and start anew."

Shela asked, "Then the events that are happening today, some people would say it is God's punishment, that isn't true?" John asked, "Doesn't it say in the bible that the angels poured out God's wrath on mankind?"

Ajh answered, "God is not punishing us. That will come later when everything is destroyed. Ask yourself this. Who created all the pollution in the air, our oceans, rivers, and streams? Who damaged the ozone layer? Who created AIDS, man did, not God."

"Remember many parts of the bible in Revelations are symbolic. For example, John was shown the future and the past. It says a star was thrown down on the water and a third of the waters became wormwood. Wormwood is bitter; this would mean polluted streams and rivers. And smoke went out of the bottomless pit and the sun and air were darkened by the smoke. This is the oil wells and because of oil, we have pollution and the green house gasses and chemicals that harm the ozone atmosphere, which will scorch man with heat and allow the sun's rays to cause grievous sores on man, which is skin cancer. In Revelations it says, "*The seas became like the blood of a dead man*", a dead man's blood is black. This would be the oil spills around the world."

"The Two Witnesses, or Two Turtle Doves, are here but it is not their time yet to do God's will. When it is time, they will prophesy and tell people to repent, spreading the message around the world and they will destroy the city of whores. And if they choose, no rain will fall upon the earth while they are doing God's will, which will be about three and a half years."

"Then the Two Witnesses will be killed by man because man still did not repent. Just as they did not believe in Jesus, or any of God's messengers, mankind will not believe in the two witnesses. And as their bodies lay in the sand, many will rejoice. But on the fourth day, their bodies will rise and be taken into Heaven. Then mankind will see the wrath of God."

"Remember, before God does this, the scriptures must be fulfilled Jesus said, "*There will be wars and rumors of wars and nation shall rise against nation and kingdom against kingdom and there shall be famine and pestilence and earthquake in diver's places,"* which means in the oceans around the world and these will be the beginning of sorrows and Christians will be killed and hated for Jesus' name sake."

"Many false prophets will arise and deceive many. And the love of many shall wax cold. The gospel of the kingdom shall be preached in all the world and you will see the abomination of desolation spoken of by Daniel, the prophet." A false christ shall come and deceive many. You must have wisdom and knowledge of the scriptures to know the truth. Jesus told you that He will come out of the sky and you will see Him from the east to the west, and all shall see Him. Beware of false prophets, they are everywhere."

"It is said, *"The womb that does not bear and the paps that do not give suck."* A womb that does not bear are the abortions of today, and now we have made it legal and this is an abomination in God's eyes. There are a few scriptures to be fulfilled and when man has done most of the destruction that is coming, then God will finish it.

And when it says, *"the stars will fall from the sky,"* this means meteors and asteroids; after all, God is not going to destroy the universe and other life forms just because mankind refuses to follow God and advance spiritually like we should. As for science, if they would look at creation and God in a new light and by showing the vast creativity of God, it would be a lot more rewarding and mankind would advance a lot faster."

Shela asked, "I have a question about other planets, space, and time?" Ajh answered, "Yes, time is not constant, the speed of light is not constant, and space is relative to thought. Only man deals so much with time, which means so little to others and nothing to God and spiritual beings." Shela was puzzled, "What!? What are you talking about!? No, never mind, I don't want to know! What I'm asking is, with all the stars and galaxies in the universe are there other intelligent life forms out there? And did they advance as we have, at the same time?"

Ajh answered, "of course, there are other intelligent beings out there. Why would God create billions of stars in our galaxy and over 400 billion galaxies in the universe, but put life on only one planet? Why would God create stars we will never see or be able to travel to? That is like creating this whole planet, but putting microscopic life on only one grain of sand."

John said, "But most people that read the bible say that God only created us." Ajh continued, "No where in the bible does it say that we are the only ones in the universe. Our bible refers to us and our past. A lot of those people John are just ignorant of God's creativity. They are old fashioned and refuse to believe that God created anyone else but them. That has been their problem from the beginning. In old times, if you believed otherwise than what the church teaches, you were expelled from the church."

"As for your question, Shela, are other life forms advanced like us? Some are far more advanced than we are, because they have learned early in their history that working together as a family they could achieve much more. Some choose to advance spiritually and live a simple life and there are others who do not advance at all, because of their mistrust of each other and the hatred and greed in their hearts, much like this world is becoming. Some look like us that are carbon base and some do not that are not of the same base, like silicone based. But all the advanced forms have at least three fingers to advance in technology, much like the thumb, index, and middle finger," as Ajh wiggled his three fingers to show them. "Of course, spiritually you only need your heart and mind to follow God and you will advance beyond all others."

John asked, "Ajh, in the bible in Revelations, all those weird looking beasts, why are they described that way? Are there beasts like that in heaven?" Ajh answered, "well, God can create any variation of animal he likes, but remember in Revelations John was given a vision of the past and future."

"Some are real; some are symbolic of the beast he thought he saw. For example, picture in your mind John in revelations coming from a time in our history with no technology 2,000 years ago. If you take this man and show him the future, how do you think he would describe a car? The headlights when they are on resemble eyes of fire. The grill, especially the old cars with chrome bars going vertically, would look like the teeth of a lion. The windows would look like eyes all around its head. If a man was driving, he would say it had the head of a man. Then in Revelations it says, "*Smoke came out of its tail.*" This would be the smoke coming out of the tail pipe to hurt mankind and the earth and "*the smoke darkens the sun and the moon.*" This again would be the pollution, smog and green house gases."

"Even the planes in World War I, they had double wings; in the bible it says, "*a great eagle with six wings,*" counting the two in the tail. As we built bigger planes, in Revelations it says, "*Their wings thundered like a 1,000 chariots or mighty waters.*" In World War I and II, man painted pictures on planes. There is a lot of machinery today that would be described as a beast especially in construction equipment with teeth to hurt the earth."

"Revelations talks of "*stars falling from the sky.*" Today we know they are meteorites and asteroids that will fall to the earth causing much destruction. "*Hail and brimstone*" could be the use of atomic bombs and even laser beams being fired from satellites could be "*fire from the sky.*" So if you look deep enough and open your mind, a lot of descriptions in the bible and what we see and know today coincide with each other. In Moses' time hail was mingled with fire. How would scientist explain that?"

Ajh paused, continued walking, and shook his head. "That almighty dollar everyone strives for more than they strive for God. It is the cause of all the problems in the world. Greed, is why people do the terrible things they do."

"If man would do away with money, no one would have any power? Everyone would be equal. Everyone would work for the good of mankind. Can you imagine if everyone only had to work 8 hours a day, 4 days a week and you can have everything you want. The world would become a paradise. Civilization would advance, no poor, no homeless, no hunger and science would be traveling through space, and we could clean up the earth, all because we have no expenses. I know this would be difficult for the world to change, but if we all prayed together, we would have one thought of wanting to be righteous with God. Our outlook would be different and we would have a common goal."

"We all have the power to vote out the corrupt politicians. It is odd that each country is controlled by a handful of powerful people. Why are billions of people subjected to the few that are rich and powerful, because of money? Without it, they are nothing. The people can retaliate in a nonviolent way for a better system. Just think if several hundred million people refused to work, use their vehicles, use electricity, or cooperate until a better system for everyone is put into action. It would put the economy at a standstill and put fear into those that are in charge."

"I believe it will be the Reborn Christians that will do this, because they seek righteousness with God. That is one reason Jesus said *"you will be hated for my name sake."* Because they will want to do what is righteous in God's eyes. Other religious leaders will follow, because they want to follow God and righteousness. Then the world will begin to change.

John said, "A lot of people will be shot if they try to start a system like that." Ajh replied, "True, but I think a lot of people would rather be shot knowing their children, family, and friends will have a better life. No one wants to see their children working their whole life and never getting ahead."

"But if you believe without doubt that no one can harm you, then you will walk the earth in a spirit of God and no one would have any control or be able to harm you. You could be healing and feeding the poor. The retched, when they see what you can do in the name of God, a great fear will come over them. Then sex, pornography, blood shed, prejudice, greed, lust, and all that is not of God will disappear; the world will finally change for the better."

"John asked, "Ajh you said something before about being able to tell when an earthquake is coming after a lot of lightning strikes, our scientist don't have that knowledge yet." Ajh answered, "They have not studied the connection between the lightning strikes and the tectonic plates. You see when the plates down below are rubbing against each other they are creating an electromagnetic field. As it builds up in the ground and when you have a storm over head you have a lot of lightning strikes. This will tell scientist that the plates are rubbing against each other and possible pressure building up. Then in a little while you will possibly have a tremor or an earthquake. Depending on how many lightning storms you have and the repeated lightning strikes, will give you and idea on how much the plates are rubbing against each other and through continuous study they will be able to determine the amount of pressure."

"Have you two ever heard of the Shroud of Turin?" They both said, "No, what's that." Ajh explained, "It is the cloth that covered Jesus in the tomb where He was buried. In Turin, Italy they have the ancient cloth. On it is the imprint of Jesus. You see when God brought Jesus back to life His Spirit and His Light filled the body of Jesus with energy and left an imprint on the cloth, a light scorching that shows the wounds and likeness of Jesus. God did this so that we as believers with all our technologies can prove our faith, and put doubt into the disbelievers. Because the cloth has endured time and fire and is still in good condition."

"The details and images are extraordinary; you can see how many times His back was whipped and how deep. The cloth showed the markings from the crown of thorns, the wounds in His wrists and feet, it showed the bruises on His face and the spear wound in His side. And it is a three dimensional image, showing depth. They could even measure the size of the spear that entered His side and punctured His heart. It also showed the bruises on His face and His knee when He fell caring the cross."

"Some people claim that an artist in the 14th century forged this painting, yet they do not know how nor can they duplicate it with all their 20th century technology. Yet the so called forger did not go along with traditional beliefs. That Jesus was pierced through the wrist, it was a cap of thorns because the thorns also punctured the top of His head, and that he was nude in the burial tomb. And His hair was in a pigtail in the back, like Rabbis wore at the time. The artist would have had to have 20th century knowledge of biology, knowledge of first century Jewish customs, first century Roman crucifixion, type of weapons they used and the coins on the eyes were issued by Pontius Pilate 29-32 A.D…."

"The image of Christ is made into a 3D image. It is a negative photograph. Another interesting fact is it had on it pollen from the Middle East and the countries from around the Mediterranean Ocean into Europe all the places it was exposed. Scientist today with all their technology can not duplicate the process or figure out how the artist did it. Their findings were that there are no chemicals, no paints, stains, powders or dyes used. The image is a complete picture of His beating and crucifixion. It also showed that His legs were not broken, which is the Roman custom. This also means the Romans were satisfied that He was dead. That is why they pierced His side with the spear to make sure He was dead. A little bit of blood came out because it punctured His heart then water, He shed all His blood. And the position of His legs means rigor mortis had set in."

"Some people say that the Apostles stole His body to make the scriptures come true. The Apostles were afraid of the people, and they were afraid of being persecuted so they were in hiding. What would make them be so brave as to go out in public and proclaim Jesus as the Savior without fear of persecution? Because they saw Him, and knew that He had risen from the dead. They knew His words were true and they were blessed with the Holy Spirit. "

"With all the evidence scientist will not admit it is the burial cloth of Jesus. Even though there is no historical evidence of anyone else being crucified in this manner. And they will never admit that the image is miraculous."

Chapter IX

Shela and John learn their first spiritual lesson

As they finished walking across the large field of grass, they came to the bottom of the rocky hill where they were heading; it went several hundred feet up. Ajh started up the hill and said, "come on, we have to climb to the top and over to the other side of this hill." They followed him up the hill and asked, "What is on the other side?" Ajh replied, "You have much to learn in a short time and you have some good spiritual lessons to learn."

It was a long ways up, it became tiresome and they were sweating a lot with the hot sun on their backs, but the higher they climbed the cooler the breeze felt. Occasionally, they would stop and rest, turn around and sit on the rocks and gaze upon the beautiful scenery. It was a clear day. They watched the grass wavering in the wind. John pointed to an eagle fling in the distance. To their left the clouds had cleared over the mountaintop and you could see the snow all the way up to its majestic peak. The bright green of the grass fields against the dark green of the tree line and the mountains, with the pale blue sky was picturesque.

After enjoying a good rest, they all decided to continue climbing. When they reached the top, it was flat ground but rocky. They took their time walking across the stones to the edge of a cliff. Looking down, they were mesmerized by the beauty of a deep gorge with two huge walls separated about fifty feet wide and several hundred feet deep and the color of the rocks within. They stood on the edge of the cliff. The wind was blowing strong. Ajh looked at them, "Remember when Jesus walked on water. He also said, "*You can do as I have done if you have faith and believe without doubt.*" Shela and John stood dazed; looking at each other, wondering what was his point.

Ajh turned and walked off the cliff. They stared in amazement. There was Ajh walking on air over to the other side. As he stood on the rocks and said, "Well, come on!" John exclaimed, "You expect us to do that!?" Ajh answered, "Have faith and believe without doubt that God is always with you."

Shela blessed herself and just walked off. John was looking around. When he saw her walking off the edge, he tried to grab her, but she was out of reach, and she made it to the other side. She was smiling and jumping up and down clapping her hands, feeling pleased with herself. They looked at John, "come on." He shook his head. "You can't be serious!?" Ajh with a stern voice, "have faith and believe!" Shela yelled out, "come on, I did it!"

John was shaking like a leaf in the wind. He kept looking at the rocks below and the huge walls of the gorge in front of him. They kept edging him on. John closed his eyes, walked off the cliff and he fell. Shela screamed and turned her head and started crying. You could hear John's scream faintly fading away echoing in the walls as he fell into the deep gorge.

Ajh stretched out his hand, "Behold." You could hear John's screams getting louder. There he was in mid air, as if kneeling on a sheet of glass. John looked up and crawled over to Shela and hung onto a large boulder. She hugged him, and was still crying. John was shaking. Ajh said, "come on, we have things to do." Ajh turned and started walking up the rocky path. They ran after Ajh. John grabbed Ajh's arm and spun him around. "I'm getting sick and tired of you! What kind of a joke is that to play on me!?" Ajh answered, "It was not a joke, it was a lesson." John, raising his voice, "You call that a lesson!? I almost got killed!"

Ajh shook his head, "you were no closer to death then, than you are right now from a bolt of lightning striking you without a cloud in the sky! Your lives are in my hands." Ajh was raising his voice and getting very stern, "and I am getting tired of telling you about a righteous path, what you should be doing to follow God and nothing is sinking in! I'm beginning to wonder why God picked you. Shela, I can see she has some potential, but you, are the most stubborn, thickheaded person I have ever tried to teach!!"

"Shela, what were you thinking of when you walked off the cliff?" Shela answered, "Well, I blessed myself and then my mind went blank." Ajh looked at John, "you had doubt, did you not!?" John said, "Yeah, I was scared!" Ajh replied, "Then you caused yourself to fall, you are not building your faith, are you?" John didn't say anything. "I am not saying you are to walk off cliffs to test God's power, because then you will fall to your death. You do not test God. Let the words of Jesus be part of you, and the Holy Spirit fill you so you know what to do. I know this kind of faith takes a while, but the more you want God in your heart; walk with Jesus, and let the Holy Spirit fill you, the easier it is to do God's work." Ajh turned and started walking up a small incline, "come on, we have work to do."

They walked behind him. Shela asked, "Why did God pick us?" Ajh answered, "Why not ask Him, He is listening?" John said, "But we are not religious people, why us?" Ajh stopped walking and turned to look at them, "because religious people are set in their ways and would argue about what is said in the scriptures. They would bounce back and forth in the bible to prove their point. Some of them change the words that they read so they can match it to another part of the Bible to prove their point. Sometimes they contradict the words of Jesus by pointing out the words of the prophets, or the apostles. Who do they really believe in?"

"They think they know what God wants, yet they say he is mysterious and they cannot answer all the questions people are asking. If you seek knowledge God will give you the answers and you should educate yourself on the latest research so you can know what the disbelievers are talking about and how to ask God for the answers. God wants people with a heart of flesh, and an open mind, not a heart of stone, and a closed mind. Use the brain He gave you. Be an intelligent child of God. Open yourself up to what he wants."

"But why us" asked John. Ajh answered, "It is in your heart to do good. You came back for me when you thought I was alive and could be seriously hurt, even though you knew you could get into trouble for it. You have come this far without turning away." John remarked, "you destroyed my bike, where was I to go!?" Ajh replied, "John, you could have walked off, but there is a deep root in both of you to follow God. It has been buried over by the ways of the world. Now is the time to let the spirit of God grow inside you. Do you think you two met by chance? God brought you two together. He brought you here."

"Shela, when you walked off the cliff your mind went blank, but what was in your heart?" She answered, "A warm feeling of confidence that God would protect me." Ajh looked at John, "see, you are not putting your trust and faith in God. He picked you two to do His will, which alone should give you both all the faith without doubt you need."

"Come, we do not have much time" as they started walking. Shela asked, "By time, you mean the end?" Ajh answered, "Yes, and also I do not have much time to spend with you. There will be destruction on this planet that mankind has never seen before." Shela asked, "How soon?" Ajh answered, "Only God knows, but I would say three, five, or maybe six years, tops. It is up to God when He decides when it is time, maybe He will delay it if He sees us turning away from our wicked ways."

John asked, "Will there be a nuclear war?" Ajh paused, "a little, there will be some nuclear weapons exchanged, mostly from small countries and terrorists. But most of the destruction will come from volcano and earthquake activity ripping open nuclear power plants and chemical plants. The effects will devastate the world. There will be a period of suffering, the sun will be darkened, and the moon will not give its light, and the days will be shorter. Then there will be signs in the sky, you will see Jesus coming and will know it is the end. Now is the time to prepare your soul for God. Do not worry about your body, it means nothing; it is your soul that is important to God. Your body is only a shell."

Shela remarked, "Ajh, it is very windy up here and it should feel very cool or cold, yet I feel comfortable, why?" Ajh answered, "God is growing in your hearts and he keeps you comfortable, and if you do not worry about the weather it will not bother you. Come on, you have a good lesson to learn."

As they arrived at the top of the small incline, they walked to the edge of a large field and sat down on a stone wall. They could see a farmer sitting on a tractor at the other end of the field plowing with a small cloud of dust behind him. Ajh said, "we will just sit here for now." Shela stood up behind Ajh and said, "The wind is making your hair blow all over the place, I'll put some of it in a braid in the back so it won't look all out of place and wild. You really need some oil in your hair." They sat on the wall and watched the farmer as he worked his way toward them. Ajh said, "Remember this throughout the day, do as you are told and say nothing, I will explain later. John and Shela remarked, "What do you mean? What are we going to do?" Ajh shook his head, "do as I say, shh!"

As the farmer came close to them, he stopped and got off the tractor. The footprints and dust showed how dry the soil was; he took his hat off and wiped the sweat off his forehead with his long sleeve shirt he had on. He was a tall, thin man, lots of gray hair, and a worn face. It showed the years of hard work and hardship.

He looked at them and said, "I could use some help and you look like you need work." He paused, "well don't just sit there, give me a hand." They all stood up, Ajh again told them to follow orders and say nothing. They both had confused looks on their faces and John was muttering, "what do we have to work for!? Ajh answered, Jesus said, *"If a person asks you to go with him a mile, go with him two."* Always be giving of yourself, serving others."

The farmer put Ajh on the tractor plowing. He put John to work chopping and stacking wood. Shela pitched hay in the barn and fed the animals. All day the farmer kept yelling at them, saying they were worthless bums and they didn't work hard enough for the money he was paying them.

About mid day John had had enough of the farmer's insults. He slammed the ax into the log, turned to the farmer and raising his voice, "look, I have had it with you!" Just then, Ajh yelled out, "John, be silent!" John looked at Ajh out in the field on the tractor; he was bottled up with anger. He gave the farmer a dirty look, grabbed the ax, and began chopping again, more vigorously but he kept his silence. The farmer asked, "What is he, your guru, and how could he hear from out there, with the tractor running?" But John didn't say anything.

The farmer's wife kept bringing lemonade out to them. She also had a worn look on her face, some gray hair, but she looked like she had a good soul. Some cloud cover came overhead; it gave some relief from the hot sun. When the woman went into the barn to see Shela, she kept apologizing for her husband's behavior.

"I'm sorry for my husband's behavior. Don't pay any attention to him." Shela asked, "Why is he so mean," as she took some sips of lemonade? The woman answered as she sat on a bail of hay, "My husband was not always this hard on people. As the years went on he became worse, especially when our son died. Now he does most of the work himself. No one wants to work for him, so we cannot farm the land the way we should."

Shela said, "It's no wonder no one will work for him the way he acts!" The woman became silent. Then she stood up to leave. Shela stopped her, "I'm sorry; I should not have said that. It must be hard on you being out here all alone." The woman looked at Shela with tears in her eyes. Shela said, "I don't know why we are here, but that man on the tractor, he is from God and I have a feeling after today your husband will be a different man."

The woman smiled, then started walking toward the house. Shela grabbed her arm to stop her, "Did you know that over the gorge and the ridge at the bottom of the hill, there are miles of grassland to feed your cattle?" The woman said, we have never seen the other side, but I think there is a long and winding dirt road through the woods to the bottom of the ridge. But it hasn't been used in years because we own some of the road and no one comes up here. I will tell my husband."

The woman walked to the house. Shela thought to herself, "He better change after today, that mean son of a ..." Suddenly she heard Ajh's voice in her head, "do not finish that sentence, judge not and ye shall not be judged." She looked around, and then looked out the window at Ajh, out in the field sitting on the tractor. He stopped the tractor, turned, and looked at the barn, "yes, I am talking to you, do not judge, and by the way, all three of us are sent to do God's will." Then he continued plowing. She went back to work with a big smile on her face and a warm feeling in her heart.

By the end of the day the farmer called them all together. His wife came out and urged him to be fair. The farmer said with a tone of anger in his voice, "woman, I know what my job is!" Then he turned to the three of them, took money out of his pocket and said, "I shouldn't be paying you much, you are a useless bunch."

Ajh held out his hand to stop him. "We do not need your money." He looked at Shela and John, "let's go." They walked away. John asked, "We are not going to get paid, what did we do all that work for?" Ajh said, "You will see." As he put his hands on their shoulders and edged them to keep walking.

The farmer yelled out, "take this money, it is yours!" Ajh turned around, "we have no use for money." The farmer asked, "Why are you doing this?" Ajh replied, "You asked us to help you, to give you a hand, and we did. We have done what you have asked of us and now we will be on our way." They continued walking. The farmer's wife said, "Won't you at least stay for supper?" Ajh turned around as he was walking, "our food comes from the words that proceed from God's mouth, but thank you anyways!"

And then they continued walking away. The farmer began to cry. His wife had never seen him like this. As the three of them came to the end of the field, they could still hear him crying, even louder. Shela felt sorry for him, "Why is he crying so much?"

Ajh put his arms around their shoulders, "congratulations you two, you have just stored your most important treasures in Heaven. You have saved that man's soul from the pits of hell. He has finally opened his eyes and heart. He has realized how mean and arrogant he has been to people; he will become a new and different man from this day forward. He will go to church on Sunday and apologize openly to the people in town and tell them that he is a new man and that he has found God. Things will be better for him and his wife." Shela said, "I'm glad for her, she seems like such a beautiful person." Ajh said, "She is a saint, any other woman would have left him by now."

John patting and rubbing his stomach, "But we could have accepted the meal it would be nice to have a home cooked meal for a change instead of bread and berries." Ajh laughed, "No, anything we accept from him, he would have regarded it as payment in full. That is why he has never learned a lesson before. Everyone would argue with him. They would curse each other and act like him, then he feels justified in his actions. John you have not eaten anything all day, are you hungry?" John thought for a moment, "You're right, we haven't eaten since this morning with the bread and berries that we had left over and I'm not all that hungry." Ajh answered, "Let God's words fill your heart and your body will be taken care of."

"Come on, there is a stream we can wash up in, then we will head into town." They walked a little and then stopped. "Is that not a beautiful sunset" Ajh remarked. The sun was going down behind some clouds. The reddish color meant it will be a warm day tomorrow. The clouds near the sun were a bright red with some orange and yellow color. After a few minutes the closer clouds to them where they were standing were a dark charcoal gray with a purple outline. They watched the setting sun as the clouds were changing colors. The sun slowly disappeared behind the mountains in the far distance.

They walked down to the creek and washed up. Then climbed up a small hill and started walking on the road heading into town. Someone came by in a pickup truck and offered them a ride. So they climbed into the back of the truck and headed towards town.

Going down the road at the outer edge of town, with the black background of the night, they could see a yellow-orangey color flashing in the sky. As they came closer, they could see a house on fire. The truck pulled over and they all climbed out. There was a lot of commotion going on, police cars, fire trucks, ambulance, and a lot of people in the street watching, some helping if they could.

As the three of them approached the house, a woman was screaming, "My baby, he is still in there, my baby. Please God, someone help my baby!!" Everyone had deep compassion for the woman as they looked at the house. But the firemen could not get near the house because the flames were so intense. They kept pouring water on the upper floor of the house where the child was supposed to be. Ajh asked the woman, "Where is he?" but the woman kept on crying, "My baby, my baby!" The husband said, "Second floor, first room to the right."

Ajh turned to Shela and John. "Which one of you wants to get him out of there?" They started mumbling and gazed at the fire. Ajh said, "You do not think of what has to be done, you just do it."

Ajh turned and walked towards the house, as he put the hood of his robe over his head, he began saying the Our Father. Shela and John looked around. No one paid any attention to Ajh as he walked into the house. But then the fire chief yelled, "Hey, what are you doing, get out of there!" Ajh took a left through the door and went up the stairs. The fire chief took a step back and sat down on the fire truck. "My God, I don't believe it! I saw those stairs collapse not more than 15 minutes ago!" But everyone could see Ajh walk up the stairs through a large picture window on that side of the house.

As Ajh came to the top of the stairs, he started to go to the room on the right, but he felt a presence to the room across the hallway to his left. He entered the left room, there under the parents bed was the little boy huddled with his stuffed bear passed out from the smoke. Ajh picked him up and covered him with part of his robe.

Everyone was watching the house as Ajh came down the stairs and out the front door. The hood over his head and the boy wrapped up in his robe, they were totally engulfed in flames. The firemen dragged the hoses toward Ajh to douse him with water. Suddenly the flames went out. No part of his robe was scorched. He walked toward the parents, bent over to put the boy down, and unwrapped him. The boy ran toward his mother and father still holding his stuffed bear. They were crying, and you could hear the joy in their voices as they were hugging the boy. Everyone began clapping and cheering the family on and saying "Praise the Lord!" as they gathered around.

A minute latter the fire chief looked around. "Where did he go, the guy with the white robe, where is he?" People started looking around. No one could see him. The mother stood up. "I didn't get a chance to thank him."

Shela and John looked at each other puzzled, why is it that nobody could see Ajh? He was walking away, but not that far, and still in sight. With the black background of the night, the light of the fire, Ajh's white robe was glowing in the dark. It should have been easy for them to see him, yet everyone kept looking around. Shela ran toward Ajh.

John turned to the mother and said, "God saved your son. Remember to thank him every day." She answered, "I will, he knows I will!" Then John ran to catch up with Shela and Ajh.

Ajh looked at John. "Very good John, you are learning" John smiled. Shela asked, "How did you walk into the fire, how is it possible?" Ajh answered, "With God anything is possible and I have faith without doubt that God will protect me. Besides, it has been done in the bible and any miracle in the bible you can do."

John asked, "Where in the bible is it written?" Ajh answered, "In the book of Daniel. Three of Daniel's friends refused to bow to a false god, so the king ordered his men to heat up the furnace seven times hotter than normal, and throw the three of them into the furnace. The fire was so hot it burnt the kings' men as they threw Daniel's friends in. The king looked into the furnace and he was amazed. Not only were the three men unhurt by the fire, but there was a fourth man walking around with them. The king called them out and they were unharmed, so the king proclaimed their God to be more powerful then all other gods." Shela asked, "Who was the fourth man in the furnace?" Ajh replied, "who else, Jesus, so that they would have confidence that they would survive the fire."

Shela asked, "How is it that the crowd couldn't see you?" Ajh answered, "Oh that is a trick some people use to hide themselves from others, by keeping the mind totally blank. Jesus used it when the crowd He was speaking too picked up stones to throw at Him. He walked right through the middle of the crowd without them being able to see Him."

"If you are unsure as to how much power you could have from God, you will find your answers and many examples in the Bible." Ajh pointed with his finger, "We have a little ways to go down the street and then there is a side street to the right where there is a homeless shelter. We will stay there for the night."

When they arrived there, the homeless were eating a late meal because everyone was talking about the house fire. Ajh gave thanks, said prayers, and they ate. Then he began preaching to the homeless about preparing their souls, repent for their sins, that the Kingdom of God was at hand and was coming very soon.

The next morning, another beautiful, warm day, the three said prayers and ate breakfast. They said their goodbyes then headed for the center of town to a little park. It had a big lawn area for people to sit on. Ajh began preaching and people started gathering around. Many recognized the white robe from the fire; they wanted to see who he was. Regardless how big the crowd was, and how softly he spoke, they could hear him because they listened with their hearts.

Some of them started asking questions, because they were hearing a way of preaching they never heard before. Someone close asked him, "How do you know these things? How do we know you are from God or someone trying to deceive us? There have been so many false prophets and you are saying there is no mystery to God?" Ajh answered, "Listen to your heart, what does your heart tell you? Does it feel good? Are you full of joy? Then you know these words are from God. My Father is your Father."

Ajh raised his voice and looked all around at the crowd. "You have been taught to fear God! How can you fear a loving God!? Do not fear Him but fear His judgment, just as you do your parents. When you were young you feared your parent's punishment and it kept you honest, straightforward, obedient, and you respected your elders. As you grew up you realized what they were teaching you and how much love you have for them now that you understand."

"I am telling you the truth, when you learn to respect God's ways and follow the path of Jesus you will understand God, you will no longer fear Him but you will give thanks to be bathed in His glory! If you think He is mysterious it is because of your closed minds and your teachings. Is it not written in the bible that in the end the mystery of

God will be revealed!? I tell you prepare your souls and repent of your sins, because the end is near!"

"Beware of false prophets, as John in Revelations took the book, ate it and in his mouth was sweet like honey but in his belly was bitter and sour. So too a false prophet's words will be sweet to your ears and stone hearts, but to your soul is bitter and sour."

The preacher said, "You call Jesus your brother. Are you saying that you are equal to Jesus?" Ajh answered, "I am not worthy to be the sand under His feet, but Jesus said, *"You are all my brothers and sisters."* I believe in His words and therefore I am His brother. Jesus also said, *"Call no one your Father except God!"* Tell me priest what do your parishioners call you, is that not blasphemy?"

Ajh looked around at the crowd, "Just think, we give Him many names, we call him God, Lord, the Almighty, Allah, Braham, Jehovah, the One, or even a Higher Power but His true name is YHWH (pronounced Yah Wah)! His name is holy, so instead we should call him Father, so that it is more personal, a closer relationship with Him, closer to your heart, where He wants to be! If you call God your Father, then you feel you have a direct communication with him, a direct link, a closeness you can feel."

"How many times have you heard preachers say you are not worthy, to do miracles because you are a sinner? Well the prophets were sinners and God loved them and did miracles through them. Because their faith was strong and believed without doubt, that what ever miracle they wanted God would give it to them. That is the key, faith without doubt. Know in you heart that God will give you what ever you ask. It will be done."

"Talk to God always and every day, not just when you go to church or when you are in trouble. He loves you; he wants to be close to you. All your troubles and burdens that are on your mind, let them go, tell God you give Him these burdens and things that trouble your mind, and from this day forward you will live your life by God's ways. If you will live a righteous life, God will take care of you, in the good times and the bad, God is always with you. The bad times comes from dealing with man, not from God."

"He is watching you and listens to every word you say. If you have questions, they will be answered, sometimes not right away or the way you expect, but if your faith is strong He will answer and it will have a very deep meaning to you so you will know the truth. All you have to do is *"ask and you shall receive, knock and the door shall be opened"*. If you want wisdom, just ask. If you want knowledge, knock and the door will be opened. Whatever you want, God will give to you. He has plans for you."

The preacher said, "you say to talk to God directly, are we to forget Jesus?" Ajh shook his head, "Did anyone hear me say this? Your anger is making you deaf preacher. I tell you, when you talk or ask God for help, always say you do this in the name of Jesus, and in the name of Jesus you thank Him, therefore you give Jesus honor. This is what Jesus wanted you to do. Without Him and His words you would be lost."

"How many times have you gone to church and hear them say over and over again, Jesus, Jesus, praise Jesus, and never talk about God, the Father? Should you not start the mass or sermon with the Our Father as Jesus commanded you to do, or break bread and drink wine to represent His body and blood? He said, *"Do this in memory of me,"* why is it done once a month or not at all."

"Jesus said that on Judgment Day there will be many that will say, *"Lord, Lord did we not prophesy in your name, and in your name cast out demons, and in your name perform many miracles?"* And Christ will say, *"I never knew you, depart from me, you who practice lawlessness."*

"Do you not know why he said this" Ajh paused and throughout the whole crowd there was silence. "Because you honor Jesus more than you do God the Father. Jesus is your savior; He showed you the way to God the Father. He shed His blood so you could be cleansed of not just your sins but your ignorance of the truth. Jesus died so you can know the truth. He took *"Love thy neighbor as thy self"* to its greatest heights when He gave up his life for you."

"This is how much love you are supposed to have for each other. Follow in His footsteps, follow his words. His words will set you free. His words will give you knowledge, wisdom and faith to do the will of the Father, and you can do miracles. Know that you are worth more than the lilies of the field, look how they are adorn, and the birds are fed. God loves you more than these and they are taken care of."

"Honor and love God the Father with all your heart and give God the credit for all the good that you do. This will show others that you are of God. And that alone can be your ministry. Let Him live in you, and keep His commandments. By doing these things because Jesus told you, you give Him honor. He said, *"not everyone that says to me Lord, Lord, will enter into the Kingdom of Heaven, but he who does the will of my Father is worthy of Heaven."* Doing and acting out the will of the Father is what Jesus meant by believing in Him and you will be saved."

"You are taught that you can not be saved by good works alone, that just believe in Jesus and you will be saved. But tell me, if you do not do good works then how are you doing the will of the Father? Did not Jesus say, *"If a person asks to go with him a mile go with him two,"* or *"If he sues you for your shirt give him your coat also, to visit them in prison, when you feed the poor you have fed Me"* these are all words of action, when you do good works you are doing the will of the Father."

"Jesus said, *"Whosoever will come after me let him deny himself and take up his cross and follow me."* These are words of action; we must follow Him in action and in love for Him. If we loose our life for the sake of Jesus and the gospel we shall be saved. For what is life, but a blink of an eye compared to eternity of joy and happiness."

"And you Christians that say if you do not believe in Jesus you will not go to Heaven. If a person believes in God the Father and obeys the Ten Commandments better than you, on Judgment Day where will he go? Will he go to hell? In the end there will only be two places to go, heaven or hell."

"Tell me if this man refused to believe in Jesus, could you tie him to a pole and whip him every day and all day until he believes in Jesus? Even with your hearts of stone you would say no. Then how could Jesus send this man to hell when he did what Jesus said to do, *"Do the will of the Father."* For hell is far worst than a whipping." Shela and John were nodding their heads.

"Ajh paused to let the people think of what he said. Then he continued, "I heard a preacher say that Gandhi would not go to Heaven because he did not recognize Jesus as the son of God. I tell you that this preacher lied, because Gandhi did what Christ told you all to do. He did the will of the Father, yet this preacher was found with a prostitute. Who then will go to Heaven? The one who says Lord, Lord to Jesus, yet his heart is far from God, or the one who does not call Jesus Lord, but his heart is with God always. I tell you judge righteous by that which is righteous. For on Judgment Day, Christ will say to Gandhi, *"I am the way and the light of the world and the Son of God, please enter Heaven."*

"Did not Jesus say that *"He who does the will of my Father is my brother and sister?"* When He was nailed to the cross the thief that was also nailed to a cross said to Jesus *"Remember me when you enter your kingdom, and Jesus said, today you will be with me in Paradise."* There are many examples in the Old Testament also that God said how to get to Heaven. Do not judge others; do not let those words of judgment come out of your mouths, for they come from your stone hearts. Because as you judge so shall you also be judged."

"There are Christian organizations converting people around the world and teaching them that Jesus is God and they are not taught about God the Father. Jesus is the Son of God and the Body of God, and like the Holy Spirit is part of God but not all of Him. They should be teaching them to love and pray to the Father; accept Jesus as their Savior, and receive the many blessings of the Holy Spirit which are the gifts and essence of God the Father. Jesus shed His blood so we could be washed of our sins and know the truth. Honor Him by spreading and telling the truth."

"Because of religious teachings people think if they believe in Jesus they will be saved. But their actions are not of God. They dress provocatively; woman exposing their breast wearing a cross, is that not blaspheme? People use the Lord's name in vain. Every other word out of their mouth is profanity. They watch TV of sex and blood, they gossip and have anger with their neighbor, and the list goes on. Then on the Sabbath in church they pray and act accordingly. Only those who do the will of the Father as often as they can will enter Heaven. For this is the way of Jesus; follow in His foot steps."

Ajh looked at the preacher, "Jesus said to give up your possessions and follow me. How many possessions do you have!?" Then he looked at the crowed, "How many can you do without!?" Ajh turned to look at the priest and said, "You yourself do not teach or follow the words of Christ, you call yourself father, when Jesus said call no one your father except God! You changed the words in the scriptures because of your teachings and beliefs! Jesus said, "*If you change one word of the scriptures, you will perish in hell.*" I tell you, your popes that have changed these words are in hell, and you pray to saints when you are to pray to God only! Some of you change a word in the scriptures so you can make a point in your sermons. This is wrong; never change a single word in the scriptures!"

"Priest you believe the Blessed Mother was always a virgin, yet Jesus had brothers and sisters, this you have removed from the bible. Even common sense would tell you, the angel of the Lord told Joseph not to touch Mary until after the child was born. It was also the Jewish belief to bring up as many children in their name, an in their Jewish faith as possible, so why would Joseph not have more children? You pray to Saints. You also pray repetitiously as Jesus told you not to do and you make up your own sins. Only if you break God's commandments then you commit a sin! Your church has many sins, you are the one that was said in Revelations that "*you are neither hot nor cold, but I' wish you would be hot or cold, but because you are lukewarm I will spit you out of my mouth."*

"And you preachers, and pastors, you are no better! You too are not doing the will of God or following in Jesus' footsteps! I rarely have heard the Our Father in your Reborn Churches, and you do not break bread or drink wine in your weekly services to honor Jesus! You say you do not want to make it a ritual where it has no meaning! The very words of the Our Father are words to live by! If you understood them you would say them every day!"

"You also never mention the Blessed Mother to give her honor. Did not Jesus, when he was nailed to the cross, say to His apostles, which is also saying to everyone, *"Behold thy mother."* "She has appeared too many with signs and messages that we all should listen to, because she has begged God for these signs to save as many of your retched souls from the pits of hell, so you would turn from your wicked ways. Your mother is looking out for you."

"I have been in your re-born churches and you talk of positive thinking toward God and you repeat the scriptures, but you do not teach the Ten Commandments and their deep meaning! You also preach the words of the apostles and prophets more than you do the words of Jesus! All the words of Jesus reinforce the Ten Commandments. I do not have to read the words of the prophets; the apostles or their actions. For the words of Christ alone ring true in my heart and enlighten my soul. Because His words came from God's mouth. The words of the apostles teach you how to be good and how to deal with the world. The words of Jesus teach you to forget the material world, how to be a spiritual being and be righteous with God the Father. His words are true, and His truth shall set your spirit free."

"You preachers do not tell the people the things they do wrong or the right TV or movies they should watch! That they should not steal, even from work where they feel they are not getting their just wages! And do not destroy other people's property! But mostly, you should teach the right way to dress! Not to dress or look provocatively to put lust in other people's hearts! Women are exposing skin, wearing skin tight clothing showing off their shape, as if they are still advertising that they are available, even in church! That goes for you men also; you walk around parading yourselves like a rooster perched on a fence post in a chicken yard! But the hawk will swoop down and pluck out your lustful heart! Dress respectfully in the House of the Lord! You came to praise Him, not to attract others. He does not care if you are dressed in rags it is your heart that should be adorned with love for Him!"

"Women, cover your bodies and men also. God said to man, *not to let a blade cut a single hair on your head.*" Do you know why God said this!? With bodies covered, heads covered and unshaved, people will look into your eyes, they will see and get to know the person you truly are! They will look within and know who has a good soul, because the eyes are the windows to the soul. If people fall in love because of the soul, this is truly a match made in Heaven. But, if you fall in love because of looks or sex, when they go, so will the love go also!"

"Too all the religious leaders, I am telling you, you should be speaking out against terrorist, and all hate groups and those that take up weapons that are part of your religion, denounce them, stand up for God! Speak out against hatred and bigotry, for God lives in everyone; if you hate them then you hate God!"

"Preachers, do you speak out against abortions or are you afraid of losing your parishioners!? I tell you that those who have abortions and fight to keep it legal, these people will be reincarnated as aborted fetuses over and over again, until Judgment Day! After all, why would God give a child in a womb a soul only to be tormented and aborted in the womb!? Why not let those who want abortions legal or have abortions, be tormented!? This will be their hell!!"

Ajh paused, "Did not Jesus say, not to divorce except in the case of adultery, yet you allow divorces in your churches. A Buddhist priest teaches their people the eight paths to God; the right view, the right intent, the right speech, the right conduct, the right means of livelihood, right endeavor, right mindfulness, and the right meditation. If you truly follow Christ, should you not teach your parishioners the same, and go beyond this to achieve a spiritual path toward God!? You mimic the words of Christ, but you do not understand Him. You should also tell your parishioners, if they are true Christians then they should stand up for God's ways when ever and where ever they go."

I say also to you preachers, there should be no exchange of money within the temple of the Lord, but outside the doors of the temple, for God does not need money in His house. The only offering you should bring to the alter is your heart and soul!"

"You preachers with your expensive churches, before you beg for money, take a look around you and how you spend the money foolishly. Look how lavishly you live and how you decorate your churches. God wants a plain building and an altar made of fieldstone and dirt, fieldstone that no tool has touched it. You see, God likes things plain and simple, no frills. You beg for money when your parishioners are poor, and yet you still go on vacations and spend money foolishly in church with elaborate decorations, TV screens, sound systems, and so on. Let us think of Godliness!"

"Some of you preachers condone homosexuality, abortions, and divorce! You are no different than the preachers that allow sexuality and mass suicide and say they are of God! You stray away from Godliness because you let the way of the world tell you what is right and wrong! The churches and temples should be on the front lines of God's army and stand up for what is righteous in God's ways! Do not step back or be afraid! If you do, then step aside and let someone else lead the people! You are either for God 100% or against God 100%, there is no middle line!"

"You must love God with all your heart and do what He wants, now is the time to decide! Have some back bone; do not let others intimidate you! If they laugh and scorn at you, then they are not your friends, but they are Satan's friends! Find those who want to stand for God and your courage will grow! You are His children, act like His children!!"

Someone close to him asked, "Who are you to say what is right and wrong and what God wants?" Ajh replied, "I was sent by God to bring you a message. I know what is in my Father's heart; I am just a lowly messenger, a lowly messenger from Heaven, a rock for my brother, Jesus, to walk on! I am not fit for his feet to touch me, but I rejoice that I am a rock in Heaven! It is better to be a stone for people to walk on in Heaven, then to endure the pain of one finger in hell!" Shela and John were nodding their heads.

"To know God you must want Him and forsake all materialistic needs. To understand God, you must destroy your ego. Think nothing of yourself, be willing to serve others and ask for nothing in return. Love everyone equally without prejudice or judgment, love sinners and your enemies just as you do your own family. If you seek joy, seek His love. If you seek happiness, let God enter your soul and heart so your whole body will be filled with His light. If you seek wisdom, understand everything and everyone around you and seek the truth. If you seek forgiveness, just ask. If you seek God's knowledge, knock and the door shall be opened."

"To be one with God, abandon your self-image and personality and accept God in you, ask Him to bless you with His Holy Spirit. So your body is filled with His Light and He may see the world through your eyes and your senses. Let God feel the wind on your face, the grass under your feet, let God into your heart so He can experience what you experience. He wants to live in you! You are but a candle of light in a large room, the more you have God in you the brighter you will be. Become a mirror of God's light and be an image of Him wherever you go and light up the world."

"If you seek His kindness, then you must have a heart of flesh and destroy your heart of stone so you can spread kindness to others, even to your enemies and oppressors. If you seek His peace, do not worry your mind of anything of this world, God will take care of you. If you seek His love, well, if you sought any of His gifts I have mentioned, you would know that you always had His love. If these things are in your heart then you will do more of God's work!"

Ajh paused, "But if you are prejudice because of race or religion or for whatever reason, you will not enter into Heaven! If you harm or are mean to animals because you think you are superior you are not going to Heaven! God created these creatures and they belong to him! "Love God and Love Thy Neighbor" are the two most important commandments! If you take God's name in vain, you will not go to Heaven! If you break any other commandment, you also break these two, which all the rest are based on! If you kill someone in the name of God, you will go to hell!" Ajh paused, and shouted "On judgment day God will take out your heart of stone and give you a heart of flesh and you will be shown all your iniquities! And you will know you do not belong in Heaven!!"

"We are not meant to have homes, cars, TV's, and all these material things. On earth as it is in Heaven. God created us to be gods on earth therefore we do not need these things, all we need is God. Nor should we eat as gluttonous people. Our bodies are able to sustain itself for days without food. Prayer and fasting will bring you closer to God. But if you will, let the words of God fill your heart and proceed out of your mouth, and your body will be taken care of. All the things we think are so important mean nothing."

"Someone asked, "Who then can be saved?" Ajh answered, "When you are born again of the spirit, you have a heart of flesh and you become like a child, only then will you see God and all your questions will be answered. A child is not prejudice, of color or religion; all they want to do is play and enjoy the world. Be like a child. Ask God for forgiveness, you will be on the right path and you will be saved."

"Read the words of Jesus, in the four Gospels, over and over again until you understand what He was teaching you, to do the will of the Father. Accept Jesus as your savior and He will show you the way. If your heart truly seeks the truth all you have to do is ask God, and He will send the Holy Spirit and your mind will receive knowledge as you read the words of God. If you sought any of the gifts I have mentioned you will be on your way."

"When you pray, pray in spirit. Know in your heart that God heard you and He will answer your prayers. Do not hope He heard you, for hope is for those that have doubt. Do not seek pride for it is the down fall of mankind. Do not be proud of your achievements for without God you can do nothing. That is why you should give God the credit for all the good you do. I know these things are hard, that is why God has given you the scriptures for instructions, because there are many examples to learn from. And Jesus wants to take you to a spiritual place beyond your expectations. Put your trust in God and nothing else."

"If you think you can get by without God's help then you have lost your way, you are not a child of God. You have lost the meaning of God. For the Father has much power and wants to spread His power to all of us. He is a loving God that wants to share His love and wealth with all of us. If you do not want His gifts or say you can get by without them, then you are no different than those who say there is no God, because they think they can get through life without God also. And do not think that God is punishing you or testing you. This is Satan's doings, because he knows in your hearts of stone you will be blaming God for all your troubles. Satan preaches that God is vindictive, angry, destructive, and punishing and testing us. Is this a God of Love? God is watching to see how well the words of Jesus are written in your heart and who among you will stay faithful."

"If you follow God and look back on your path before you will see how far you were from the truth, and God. Just continue forward, your past is a guidance not to be repeated. Look forward into the light; continue to take whoever you can along with you. God has given you gifts from the Holy Spirit, use them for His purpose. Ask God to show you what they are. It could be your job, that you are a blessing to others. Even the little things you do, is a blessing to others. If you are a musician play and sing for God. The money you make help the poor and starving. If you are an actor stand fast in God's ways and do not take part in shows or movies that are not of God. Use your gifts to do His will and help mankind find God. And profess to others the gifts God has blessed you with so the word may be spread."

"He can bless you with as many gifts as you want. Do not be a servant that Jesus spoke of, which is given much by his master but, hides the money and does nothing with it to return to the master. For what use is this to God. He wants you to use your gifts to prosper and help each other. God has great power that He wants to share with you; He wants you to use His power to do good. Goodness comes from knowing God."

"We are born with love. Because our soul that we are born with came from God, our soul is part of God and God is Pure Love. Jesus came to show us what true love from God is and to put us back on the right path. We must follow Him and spread love to others. And say to yourself, I have no enemies, they are my brothers and sisters that have strayed from God, it is my place to bring them back to God."

A policeman made his way through the crowd. "What are you doing here?" Ajh replied, "I am telling them about God." The policeman said, "Sorry, you are on public land. We have strict rules about separation of church and state." Ajh turned to the crowd, "Are we not one nation under God? And was this country not founded on the beliefs of God?" Everyone shouted "Yes!!"

Ajh turned to the police officer, "Maybe you are right about separation of church and state, but God and state never. He raised his voice and turned to the crowd, "Any country that does not acknowledge God and follow his laws will fall." Ajh paused, "think back, ever since the 1960's you have been taking God out of your schools, out of your courtrooms, and some people are trying to take it out of the country and out of your lives. Ever since then your country has been slowly falling apart. Bring God back and your country will be healed." Everyone began clapping and cheering. Ajh turned to the policeman, "I am not teaching them about a religion, but about God, a being who does exist."

Just as the crowd was silent, there was a screeching of tires in the street; everyone turned to see what happened. A little boy named Tommy was running out in the street crying and screaming, "no, no, my dog, my dog!!" Everyone gathered around to see the dog that lay in front of the car. The butcher, who came out of his shop to listen to Ajh speak, took off his apron and covered the dog. The boy's father pulled him away and hugged the boy.

Ajh made his way through the crowd and he knelt beside the dog and said to the boy, "son, come here. Your dog is alright. Come and see." Everyone mumbled and made sounds of disgust. The butcher asked, "What is wrong with you!? Have you any feelings for the boy!? He feels bad enough, don't play tricks on him!" Ajh replied, "*suffer the children not, for theirs is the Kingdom of Heaven.*" "Come here boy." The boy started to go but his father held him back. Ajh pulled the butcher's apron off the dog. The dog got up and ran to the boy licking his face. The boy was shouting for joy and hugging the dog.

Everyone was stunned and mumbling to each other, "how can he bring a dog back to life? It's an animal." Ajh shook his head, "Why do you mumble amongst yourselves? Do you think there are no animals in Heaven? If a child asked God for a pet, do you think God would say no? Tell me; is it not righteous to give the child his pet or to watch him suffer? See things with your heart and make your heart a temple for your Heavenly Father. If you do this, then God will work miracles through you."

"Everyone can do miracles if you believe and have faith without doubt that is the key. You do not doubt God heard you or will answer your prayers, you know He will. All you have to do is follow Jesus on a path toward God, and do the will of the Father. Ajh paused and spoke louder, "God wants you to use His powers to help each other! That is why there are so many problems in the world, because you have lost your faith! You are all his children! Be righteous and loving in God's ways! It is time to be enlightened!"

"Everything I taught you today comes from the words of Jesus and God. Jesus was trying to teach you how to become a spiritual being and return to the Father. Is it hard!? Yes it is, only because you know of a material world and you refuse to give it up! Once you choose to be a spiritual being it becomes so easy to do the will of the Father! Jesus will be there to help you! The Holy Spirit will bless you so that you can help others with your gifts! God the Father will open many doors for you and you will see the light!"

Ajh paused again, "Go on your way and remember what you have seen and heard today, let it take seed in your heart and let your heart grow towards God! The more you think of God and His ways, the more you will want to be close to Him! And you will care less of the material world! God has blessed you all with gifts, seek them out, and use them to help each other! *"Love thy neighbor as thy self,"* is very important, it will bring you closer to God and it will open your eyes!"

"When you wake up in the morning think of God and His love for you. During the day, open your eyes to the beauty God created, and give Him the credit for all the good you do! When you go to sleep, thank Him for the day! If you do these things for God you will truly be on the right path! For God is the River of Life, He flows through us all, drink from God's water and be healed! Prepare your souls and peace be with you!"

CHAPTER X

AJH, SHELA, AND JOHN MEET MAMA

Everyone started walking away, when a heavy set, black woman with a smile that would melt your heart came up to Ajh and said, with a slight southern hillbilly accent, "Do ya have a place ta stay?" Ajh answered, "No, wherever God leads us." The woman said "I'd be right proud if ya could come inta my house, we don't have much room or much food, but."

Before she could finish what she was saying, a man in a business suit interrupted and said, "I have plenty of room and food and I think you would be a lot more comfortable at my place. You could meet the mayor and other important people." Shela and John both said, with a tone of disgust in their voices, "no, we would enjoy being with her!" The man said, "Well, that's just fine, because I didn't ask you." Then Ajh said, "We are a team, besides important people know nothing of the ways of God. They only know the ways of the world. This woman asked us from her heart, you ask so you can have prestige with your friends." The man grunted and walked away feeling insulted. Ajh looked at Shela and John. "You should not have answered him with that tone of voice, always be humble and try to be polite."

The woman said, "I didn't know these two people were with you. I don't have much room or food, we're very poor." Shela put her arms around the woman's shoulders. "Don't worry, we will have plenty. John said, "Yeah, maybe with some left over." Then Shela and John laughed. The woman said, "But I don't have much room." John answered, "Then we'll sleep outside under the stars." The woman answered, "But, where we live up in da hills, it gets very cool at night." John smiled, "when you have God's light in you, you feel warm all the time."

Ajh looked at Shela and John and smiled. Everything he has been teaching them has been sinking in and they smiled back at Ajh. Everyone piled into the woman's old, black, beat-up pickup truck, sitting on tubes and tires. She had four kids, two young boys and two little girls. The truck sounded like it wasn't going to make it. They lived quite a ways from town, up in the hills, over a bumpy dirt road. Jacob the oldest said, "The tubes and old tires are to sit on and cushions the bumps and its fun." The others said yeah and laughed.

Ajh sat in the back of the truck with Shela and John and the kids. The other bucket seat in Mama's truck was broken off and there was nothing there, just a board to cover the area. That is where Mama stored her groceries when she goes shopping.

While they were bouncing around in the back of the truck, Ajh asked Shela and John "did you two sense something about the woman when she came up to us?" They both answered, "Yeah." Shela said, "A feeling like I already know her and a deep seated feeling of goodness coming from her, almost like she has a good soul. There is something spiritual about her." John said, "Yeah, I felt that too. I also felt something about these two little girls." Ajh said, "Good, always go with your feelings. The Holy Spirit is showing you someone to pay attention to. The girls are also going to be special and grow with the spirit of God in a few years from now." Ajh leaned back and hung onto the truck. They continued bouncing up into the hills, it was a long ride.

They finally arrived at the house. It was a broken down home, in need of a lot of repairs. It was a light green color with dark green trim, but much of the paint was peeling off, a few shingles missing on the roof, and some of the gutters were missing. There were a few big trees in the yard, the only place for shade, a picnic table, small outside fire place, and a lot of open land all around the house.

They all helped carrying the groceries. As they walked on the porch, you could notice the loose boards, there were poles here and there holding up the porch roof. As they walked into the house, the inside wasn't any better then the outside. There was one light bulb hanging in the middle of the room by the wires, an old refrigerator, and an old-fashioned wood stove to cook on. As Shela and John looked around, the woman said, "it's not much, but we call it home." Ajh smiled, "then we shall call it home too." The woman smiled from ear to ear with a tear in her eye. Ajh asked, "Do you mind if we call you Mama?" The woman still smiling with tears flowing down her cheeks, "I'd be right proud if ya did, everyone up here in da hills calls me Mama." Then they hugged each other. Mama, wiping the tears from her face, said, "I'd better get goin fixin supper before it gets too late." She started preparing supper with the supplies she bought in town. She said to her oldest son, "Jacob, go milk the cow, we're goin to need more tonight." Jacob replied, "The cow's not givin much milk, ma. Don't know how much I'll get out of her."
Ajh said, "We can have water, it is what God gave mankind to clean our bodies of impurities." Shela and John walked over to Ajh and whispered, "Aren't you going to give them some food, they don't have much?" Ajh said, "Be patient, we will take one step at a time."

Her youngest son, Jackson, began playing the harmonica and Mama began singing a beautiful bible hymn. When they finished, Ajh grabbed the guitar hanging on the wall. He tuned it up, and played a song he made up. When he finished the song, Mama commented, "I like that song. It has a lot of deep meaning and good words to it."

Mama's two young daughters, Jennifer and Jasmine, came up to Ajh and asked him, "do you know all about God?" Ajh replied, "as much as he tells me." The girls asked, "Why did God kill our daddy?" Mama said, "hush girls, he just took him ta Heaven." The girls snapped back, "that's the same thing, and now we don't have a daddy!" Ajh hung the guitar back on the wall and said, "Come here and listen closely. As they sat on Ajh's lap, I want all of you to hear this. That is a lie you have been told, that has been passed down for thousands of years. You all have to know the truth."

"God does not take life away. God is life. God gives life, but very seldom, if ever, takes it away. It is the ignorance of God's ways that causes death." Mama said, "He died of cancer." Ajh continued, "Cancer is caused by the impurities in our system. God created a clean world with clean air which helps to vitalize your body with ions and clean water to clean your body and help add oxygen to your system. Today we have poor air quality, chemicals in our water and food, and chemicals we put all over our body. This brings our system down. The body is constantly cleansing your system and it cannot keep up with the amount of impurities we put in."

"And most illnesses can be cured by oxidizing the body through breathing exercises, fasting, eating vegetarian food, and clean water. Even AIDS can be cured in this way, by adding clinical form, hydrogen peroxide #35 to your water, only a few drops per glassful. And use one of those purifiers that ionize the air, while doing breathing exercises."

"Cancer, AIDS, and other viruses usually thrive on a low oxygen system. Fasting will allow your system to catch up with cleaning out the impurities in your body. Of course, our bodies were not meant to have smoke in our lungs or alcohol or anything excessive, not even food."

"But, asking God to heal you with complete faith and belief without doubt is the best way. You can meditate on God's light traveling through your body, killing all infections, diseases, or whatever ailments you have. Allow God's light to live in you always and he will keep you healthy, but that also means you live a pure life of Godliness."

"It is our fault why we die so young. God said he gave mankind 120 years to live. There is an eastern religion that says God gave us a certain number of breaths and how we use it is up to us. Instead of learning to calm ourselves down so that we breathe slower and calm the mind to live longer, we find ways to hyper our system. Everyone is in a hurry. People smoke cigarettes with nicotine that acts on the nerves. They drink soda and coffee with caffeine, which kills vitamin B, which is good for the nerves. All this hypes up your body and agitates the mind."

"To think logically and to have wisdom, the mind must be calm and clear. This is why fasting helps clear the mind. So you see it is our fault we listen to mankind and die so young. And Satan wants you to die early while you are young, foolish, and reckless, because it is at a time in your life when you think you are on top of the world and God is far from your heart, and if you die, Satan has your soul in hell and that is all he cares about."

"In the meantime, everyone blames God and the so-called mysteries of God's ways, but that is a lie. If you become close to God and ask him for knowledge, he will show you and open your mind and heart and you will know the truth. Then there are no mysteries, just the truth."

Mama asked, "what about arthritis? Myself and a lot of folks up in da hills have arthritis." Ajh answered, "Arthritis can be cured by a proper diet and by watching our habits. Throughout our lives we put our bodies through a lot of bumps, bruises and excessive strain. All this hard work is not what God intended for us."

"I was told once by a young man that he had crippling arthritis and his father had money to buy the best doctors money could buy. One day he was at the docks with his father's boat and having difficulty picking up a five gallon can of gas. The fisherman that took care of the docks asked him what was wrong with him, so he explained. And told him that even on damp days, he could not get out of bed. The fisherman said do you want me to fix you. The father and son laughed, but the fisherman was serious. The young man agreed. The old man took him to his shack, sat him in a chair and hooked a small amount of electricity to him. The father was in a panic, but the son said at this point dad, I will try anything. The old man said the electricity will crack the excess calcium deposits around the bones. Then he put him in a vibrating machine and said this will break it up. In about a month you will urinate the broken up calcium deposits out of your system and you will begin to feel better. After a month he was feeling so much better that they put the mother in the car because she also had crippling arthritis. But when they arrived at the docks the old man had died and they threw out everything he owned. When he told me this it was raining out, he drove his car to my store, and wiggled his fingers as a jester how much movement he had. The customer that I was talking to before the young man walked in was almost in shock. Because he worked for his father and knew them both personally and said that on damp days he did not go to work, and was laid up in bed.

Ajh looked at Mama, "You should take 500 mg. of magnesium. This helps dilute the calcium deposits and spreads it evenly throughout your body, especially if you eat or drink a lot of dairy products. And Glucosamine is also good for your joints."

"Whether it is science's technology or God that heals people if they continue too dwell on their problems, it will come back and will not be healed. That is why medication works on some people and not for others. They dwell too much on their aches and pains, and will not let go. The subconscious is continuously being programmed that they have these aches and pains. As it says in the bible, *the thing I feared most has come true.*"

"So you see children, God did not take your dad's life. It is the path we have chosen, to follow mankind, polluting the earth and our bodies; this is what causes diseases. We are all ignorant of God's intentions, His laws, and way of life. He gave us a clean world it is very important to keep it that way. The two little girls stared at Ajh with an expression on their face like, what are you talking about?"

Mama yelled, "Supper's on, let's gather round the table." The kids were excited and rushed to their seats; they were hungry. As they all sat around the table, Ajh gave thanks. "Father, thank you for the food you have given us, let us pray that all people on earth will eat as well as we do" and everyone said "Amen."

Everyone started digging in. Mama spoke out "Boy, I wish dat was true, dat there were no starvation in da world." Ajh asked, "How do you get by way out here?" Mama said, "We have chickens, a cow, the boys go fishin a lot, but every year there are less fish in the streams and ponds. My husband useta provide good for us, he was a hard worker till he got laid off. Then afterwards he got sick, but everyone in the hills helps each other out da best dat we can." Ajh asked, "There are others up in the hills in the same predicament as you?" "Sure are" said Mama, "some even worse off."

Ajh leaned back in his chair, "Then why not have a big party tomorrow with lots of food. We will invite all the people in the hills. Mama said, "Lord knows that I've prayed for some way to feed these people in the hills. I've seen terrible things cause of lack of food and no money for doctors." John was smiling, "Then your prayers have been answered." Shela became excited, giggling, and tapping her feet on the floor. She knew what was about to happen.

Ajh looked at Mama. "Why don't you feed them that big turkey you have in the refrigerator?" Mama looked at Ajh like he was talking nonsense. "I know I ain't got a turkey in there. Da refrigerator is mostly empty and I haven't had turkey in over a year and dat was only cause my truck hit it on the road." Ajh said, "Then why not eat that one." Mama pointed her fork at Ajh, while she was chewing on her food as if to get stern with him. Ajh shook his finger back and forth and then pointed to the refrigerator.

Mama got off the chair. "I'll prove it to ya" as she walked over to the refrigerator. Shela was getting excited. She wanted to see the expression on Mama's face. Mama said, as she was opening the door, "I know I ain't got no tur tur!" Mama slammed the door shut. The look on her face was hard to describe, like being surprised, happy, and seeing a ghost at the same time.

She flung the door open so everyone could see inside; everyone screamed and cheered with laughter. The kids squealed with excitement. The refrigerator was full of food. Mama screamed, "Praise the Lord, praise the Lord!!" Then everyone else joined in "praise the Lord!!" Everyone was laughing, jumping for joy, and began hugging each other.

Ajh said, "We can have some cake and pastry, I love chocolate chip cookies and Shela can help you." Mama said, "But I don't have the fixins for dat." Ajh smiled, "why not look in the cupboards." Mama looked at Ajh and then at the cupboards. Tears of joy were running down her cheeks. She walked over to the cupboards very slowly. She reached for the doors and then hesitated. She quickly opened the door, the cupboard was full. She jumped and screamed. Each door she opened she would jump and scream. Mama was full of tears of joy as she dropped to her knees and shouted, "Praise the Lord, thank you God, thank you!!"

Everyone was praising God. The kids were very excited and screaming. Ajh walked over to Mama and picked her up off the floor, she threw her arms around him as they hugged each other. Tears of joy were flowing down Ajh's face too. Ajh looked in Mama's eyes, "remember this always, as you freely receive, then shall you also freely give." Mama said, "Then I'll give till the whole world is fed!" Ajh smiled, "you are truly blessed with the Holy Spirit."

She gave Ajh another big hug. They all settled down to return to the table to finish eating. They were all very excited. When they were done eating, Shela and Mama did the dishes. John and Ajh helped clean the table. When they finished the dishes Mama said, "Well, we better get ta bed, we gotta get up early to start cookin. Jacob, you and your brother, Jackson, will have to get up early ta spread the word to everyone in the hills, so they will be here by da time dinner is ready. John said, "I can drive the truck, it will get us around quicker." Ajh said, "Before we go to sleep, we should say our prayers to give thanks to God for all the blessings he has given us, they all held hands and bowed their heads."

Ajh began with the Our Father and they all said it with him. *"Our Father which art in Heaven, hollowed be thy name. Thy Kingdom come, thy will be done in earth, as it is in Heaven. Give us this day our daily bread, and forgive us our debts as we forgive our debtors, and lead us not into temptation, but deliver us from evil. For thine is the Kingdom and the power and the glory forever. Amen."*

"There is a new prayer I would like to teach you, repeat after me. "Dear Jesus, Son of God, our Savior, my Brother, He who was crucified for my salvation and the Father raised Him from the dead. He who spoke the truth of all things. Jesus, who in my darkest hours, provides light. I am asking the Father in your name to forgive me of all my sins, as I forgive those who have sinned against me. And to bless me with the Holy Spirit so that my eye will be single and my whole body will be full of His light. And every day and in every way I will uphold the Ten Commandments and your words dear Jesus, will be written in my heart and unto my last breath I will do the will of the Father. Amen."

Mama was the first to speak. "I like dat prayer; it has a lot a meaning." Ajh said, "Actually it is almost the same as the Our Father, but you are talking to God through Jesus. It is like thanking Jesus for showing you the true path toward God through the words Jesus taught us. Remember all the good you do and all the things that are good, you give God the Father the credit for. And Jesus will speak highly of you when you stand before God and Jesus, on Judgment Day."

"Well, we have a big day ahead of us tomorrow. Good night, God bless, and pleasant dreams." Everyone said good night and went to sleep. The three of them went out to the barn and slept in the hay. It was a lot more comfortable than sleeping outside and quite warm if you covered yourself in hay.

The next morning Mama woke up real early, before sunrise, and started preparing food. Later on Shela woke up and walked to the house. Mama said, "You can go back ta sleep child. I can start on this alone." Shela answered as she was yawning, "No, it's alright. I always feel like I've had a good night's sleep, ever since we've been with Ajh. How long have you been up?" Mama said, "A while, I couldn't sleep much, I'm so excited."

Then Mama asked, "How didja meet him?" Shela started to explain how they first met. Then she sat down and started crying. Mama said, "What's wrong child?" Shela answered, "three days ago I wouldn't give two cents to listen to someone preaching about God, but what I have seen and felt in my heart in the past few days, I wouldn't trade for the world. My life has been changed, now I don't want to live without God. I don't know why he chose me, but I'm glad he did." Shela and Mama had tears in their eyes. Mama walked over to Shela and hugged her; "dat's why he picked ya. Now tell me, what sort a things have ya seen in the past few days?" So she told her everything, right from the beginning.

About a couple of hours later Jacob woke up, then he woke up Jackson, and went to the barn to get John. "Come on John, we got a lot of ridden ta do." The kids ran to the truck and threw more tires and tubes in the back. John looked puzzled, "Why more tires?" Jacob said, "These dirt roads out here are really bumpy and it makes it fun, sometimes you have to hang on goin over the bumps." John had a big smile on his face. Then he got in the truck and they headed up the hills.

Mama ran out the door and shouted, "Jacob, tell da Thompsons and da Parkers ta bring their picnic tables and chairs and everyone bring deir own dishes!" Jacob yelled back, "okay Mama!" All the yelling woke up the two little girls. They got dressed and went out to play.

Ajh stood in the barn to milk the cow. Shela ran out of the house. "Ajh, Ajh!" He walked to the barn door. "We forgot to tell John to ask for ice from everyone for the drinks!" Ajh yelled back, "okay I will tell him!" Mama asked her, "How can he tell John when he's already gone!" Shela smiled, "Ajh has ways."

She continued telling Mama about her experiences with Ajh. Mama asked, "What did Satan look like?" Shela said, "He was horrible. First his face was deformed with bumps and molds and horns, he kept changing his face. Then he made his face look like mine, but with an evil look to it and he kept changing it. That really frightened me to see myself that way. It was like showing me what I was like, or would become without God. Hell was terrible and so much pain, look what I did to my wrist."

Meanwhile John was bouncing his way through the hills telling the people to bring their own dishes and there will be plenty of food as he collected ice. He said "God is providing the food." Everyone had the same look on their face. Who is the stranger driving Mama's truck, but Jacob and Jackson assured them there will be plenty of food. John continued through the hills and the kids had a good time in the back of the truck. He spread the news and told them to bring their instruments and ice. Then they headed back to Mama's house, the truck bouncing and backfiring all the way.

Back at the house, Ajh walked in with two big jugs filled with milk. "Where do you want me to put the milk?" Mama turned around, "oh my goodness, dat cow has never given dat much milk! We don't have any room in da refrigerator." Ajh looked around, "I will find a cool spot until someone shows up with ice and a cooler."

Ajh was outside in the shade under a big tree, sitting on the picnic table, when some people started to arrive. He introduced himself and then he helped set up the picnic tables and lawn chairs they brought and he put the milk in the coolers they brought with ice.

John arrived back at the house. The kids jumped out of the back. He pulled some bags of ice out of the truck and looked at Ajh. "I believe you asked for some ice!?" Ajh answered, "The cooler on the left with the milk jugs has plenty of ice. Put it in the other cooler, we will use that ice for our drinks." John said, "Boy, I heard you loud and clear, like you were sitting in the truck yelling in my ear. You scared the hel--, I mean heck out of me."

Ajh laughed, "When you learn more about God, you will also learn to use more of your mind and the abilities God gave you. Some preachers teach it is wrong to use such abilities, but that is ignorance, because why would God give you a brain with 100% potential, but use less than 20%. That is a sin"

The people that showed up could hear Ajh, so they gathered around him to listen. "If you use these abilities for selfish intent, then that is evil. Or to say you receive these abilities any other way, except as a gift from God, that is wrong. You have a powerful mind, use it to better mankind, but also be a good Christian and use your wisdom that God gave you. Use your talents and ideas to help mankind, not to make money. God will take care of you. To be a good Christian, one must read the four gospels over and over again and ask God, to show you the meaning of the words of Jesus, and He will show you. Each time you read it, you will have a deeper meaning and more understanding of the scriptures. It will surprise you how simple the truth really is, and how the words are meant for everyone."

"Preachers do not understand, so they say God is mysterious, but as you become closer to God you will understand Him, and everything will fall into place. You will know what God wants and you will prepare your soul. We must spread the truth about God and His love for us, use His powers to help others and to save as many souls as we can, the time of judgment is close."

Mama and Shela came out on the porch for a breath of fresh air. It was very hot in the house with all the cooking they were doing. It was a beautiful, warm day with a slight breeze and clear skies. They walked over to the picnic tables to meet everyone.

Mama looked around and said, "Marsha, where's Jeremy?" Marsha replied, "He knows there is goin to be a lot of dancin and the kids will be runnin around and playin. He felt bad and out of place, so he didn't want to come." Ajh overheard Marsha, "What is wrong with the boy." Marsha answered, "He's in a wheelchair, and can't walk." Ajh said, "Then go and bring him here. We will have to get him out of that wheelchair." Marsha hesitated and looked at her husband Matthew.

Then Mama shouted, "Go, go get him, da Lord has come, it's time to rejoice, alleluia!"

Bill stood up. "Can I get my father, he has cripplin arthritis, and he wasn't feeling good this mornin?" Before Ajh could answer, Mama shouted "Go, go get him, dere's goin to be a miracle here taday!!" Shela smiled and put her arm around Mama. "You can feel it too." Mama shouted, "Lord, yes!" They turned around and headed for the kitchen to check on the food. Some of the women followed them to the house to help out.

When they went inside, Mama said, "I wish I had some brown sugar and honey. I can make a nice sauce to spread over da turkey." Shela said, "Second cupboard to the right, top shelf." Mama looked. "How'd dat get dere? I looked in da cupboard before and it wasn't dere. Didja do dat?" Shela smiled with tears in her eyes, "I guess so, the thought came to me, and so I told you where to find it. I believed it was going to be there. I guess what Ajh said is sinking in. Believe without doubt and have faith."

Meanwhile, John went with Matthew in his pickup truck to get Jeremy. On the way John was going over in his head the things that Ajh had taught him in the past few days and was in deep thought when they arrived at the house. Matthew said, "We can carry him to the truck and put the wheelchair in the back." John didn't say anything, he was just staring, his mind was on God and a strong feeling was coming over him. He was starting to shake a little.

When they entered into the house, Matthew walked over to Jeremy to pick him up. Matthew looked at John, "well, come on." John was shaking and the feeling growing stronger inside. He couldn't hold it in anymore. "Wait!" John yelled, he couldn't control his emotions anymore. They both looked at John puzzled.

John looked at Jeremy, "Stand up!" Matthew said, "What is wrong with you, you know he." John held out his hand as if to silence Matthew. Then again he said "stand up!" Matthew said to his son, "Do as he says." Jeremy said, "But dad, you know I can't walk." John shouted again, "Stand up and walk toward me!" Jeremy tried. He put his feet on the floor and he lifted himself up with his arms, he was shaking, his legs were wobbly at first, but he pulled himself up and he was standing.

"Dad, dad look, I'm standing!" John said, "Now walk toward me." Jeremy started to and said, "I can feel strength buildin in my legs. Dad I can walk!" He was bursting with joy, as he turned to his father, "can you believe it!? Matthew hugged his son with tears coming down his face, at the same time shaking John's hand, "thank you so much." John said, "Don't thank me; God did it, not me." But John sure felt good inside.

They were in the truck driving back to Mama's house. Matthew asked John. "Do all three of you have this power?" John answered, "All people on earth have this power. You have to have faith and belief without doubt and be as close to God as you can. All the way back to the house, in the front seat of the pickup, Jeremy hung onto John's arm."

When they arrived at Mama's house, Jeremy jumped out of the truck and ran over to his mother, "mom, mom, I can walk, look!" Marsha hugged him as she started to cry, everyone was jumping and cheering with joy. Shela, Mama, and the rest came out to see what all the commotion was about. They ran over to the picnic tables and starting cheering, "Praise the Lord!"

John walked over to where Ajh and Shela were standing, and said "I feel so good inside. When we were driving up there, I kept getting a feeling that I was to heal the boy. I thought it was my own ego, but the feeling kept getting stronger until I could not fight it anymore, I began to shake. Ajh shook his head, "you do not fight it, just let it flow through you, to do what is righteous. That was the Holy Spirit of God that you felt making you shake. Congratulations, you were stubborn in the beginning but you are coming along just fine," as Ajh put his hand on John's shoulder. Shela put her arms around John's neck and whispered in his ear "I'm so proud of you."

While the commotion was going on Bill arrived with his father. It took a while for them to get the father out of the truck and over to Ajh. Ajh looked at Shela. "I believe it is your turn." Shela walked over to the old man, she didn't know what to do. She could feel the spirit growing inside of her. She knew normally you stretch out your hand and say be healed, but that is not what she was feeling. Instead, she walked over to him and hugged him, and could feel his pain then she also felt the Holy Spirit flow through her into the old man, and suddenly the pain was gone. The old man started jumping up and down, holding on to Shela. He shouted "I'm cured, I'm cured, let's dance!" He gave Shela a kiss on the cheek and thanked her. Everyone again was praising the Lord. They started playing the instruments and dancing.

Mama went into the house to check on the food and came right back out and yelled, "no dancing yet, it's time ta eat." Shela and some of the others went into the house to carry out the food. The picnic tables were all full. Everyone sat down and they thanked God for the food he provided and the healings and began eating until they were full. The kids sat on the grass and ate.

Then Mama and the others brought out deserts. Everyone was glad to eat a good meal, they didn't expect deserts. Mama brought over to Ajh chocolate chip cookies. She said, "Eat dese first. I overcooked the last batch and they are burnt on da bottom." Ajh said, "Oh, that's great. I love them nice and crunchy with burnt bottoms. My mother, Therese, God Bless her soul, forgot them in the oven once and I have loved them like that ever since, so she would always make a separate batch for me burnt on the bottom." Ajh dipped them in his milk and almost ate the whole burnt batch.

They started playing their instruments and dancing, even Ajh got up and danced. When he was done, he sat down on the end of the picnic table across from Peter, the construction worker, who also lived up in the hills. Peter said to Ajh, "you should be here in a couple of days there will be a full moon. Up in these hills, the moon looks so big and full, it is beautiful. You'd love it."

Just then Mama bent down to pick up something she dropped. Ajh said, with a smirk on his face, "I see what you mean, the moon does look very big up close," as he patted Mama on the butt. Everyone started laughing. Mama turned around quickly with her eyes squinting and a stern look on her face. "What didja say?" Ajh got up, held his hand out in front of Mama to keep some distance and then started running. Mama was right behind him.

Ajh at first ran around the picnic tables. He said, "hey, you can run pretty fast." Mama, still right behind him said, "what, for a fat woman, I'll give ya fat when I get my hands on ya!" Ajh darted off into the field and yelled, "Mama, you're going to have a heart attack, slow down!" Mama yelled back, "I'll give ya a heart attack when I sit on ya!" Ajh yelled, "oh no, not that!" Everyone was laughing and couldn't believe how fast she could run.

Ajh was about to pick up speed when Mama reached forward and grabbed a hold of his robe that was blowing in the wind behind him. She stopped quickly and yanked back on the robe. Ajh rolled backwards on the ground, head over a couple of times. It was the funniest thing you have ever seen. She stood in front of him and said, "You give up or do I sit on ya!" He was out of breath. "No, no, you win, I give up!" You could hear everyone cheering for Mama. Ajh stood up and they hugged each other. Mama, still out of breath, "boy, I'm glad I caught ya when I did. I don't think I couldda gone much farther."

As they were walking, Ajh stopped and turned to her and said, "I have to be leaving. I have more of God's work to do." Mama moaned, "Oh" she was so disappointed. Ajh continued, "I want you to remember as you freely receive, you must freely give." Mama smiled "if God supplies, I'll give till da day I die." Ajh said, "I know, that is why you were chosen and God will give you many blessings." They hugged and walked with their arms around each other back to the picnic tables.

Ajh walked over to Shela and John, "come with me, I have to go." Shela said, "Ah, we just started to have some fun." Ajh said, with a smirk on his face, "you can come back, but I have to be on my way and I have to talk to you two alone." He said his goodbyes, and as they walked away everyone kept waving bye. Mama had tears in her eyes. She hated to see him go.

All three of them went over a small hill and out of sight. Ajh said, "Well, it is time to say goodbye." Shela said, "Where are you going?" Ajh replied, "I have to go where God wants me to do His will. It is time you two start on your own journey, preaching the word of God and the coming of Judgment Day. Teach the people to prepare their souls and to do the will of the Father. Teach them the words of Jesus. Heal the sick, feed the poor; tell them that they are all God's children and they can do miracles too if they have faith and believe without doubt. They are a channel for God's power."

"Tell them they should never stop forgiving their enemies or oppressors, not just seven times but seven times seventy; they should be like their Father, with unending love and forgiveness." Shela asked, "Are we ready to do all that? Do we know enough?"

Ajh answered, "You know enough, your faith is very strong now. You have a better understanding of what God wants. Here are two bibles to refer too. Be familiar with the entire book, there are many examples for you to learn from. It is filled with the wisdom of the ages, miracles, and the words of Christ. Believe that Christ is your Savior; He will always be with you. Remember Christ said, *"If you believe without doubt you can throw a mountain into the sea and it will be done."* You must have faith that God is channeling that much power through you. God, Himself, chose you two, so you should know deep in your soul you have His power. Read Psalms 23 and 91 for confidence."

"There will be preachers of all types that will question you about the scriptures, what you are teaching others, even question the miracles. They are the Pharisees that crucified Jesus. Do not prepare yourself on what to say against your oppressors, for when it is time to speak, the Holy Spirit will speak through you and give you wisdom and it will silence their tongues."

Now it is time for you to be baptized in the Holy Spirit, the gifts, grace, and essence of God to fulfill His work. Suddenly there was an aura around them and tongues of fire over their heads. They started smiling from ear to ear. Tears of joy were flowing down their cheeks. They started jumping up and down saying "Praise the Lord! Thank you God! Thank you!"

John said, "Why this is incredible, the feeling is hard to describe! I feel like I am full of energy, love, and confidence! I feel at peace! I feel like running!" Suddenly John darted off running at full pace with bible in hand. Shela yelled out "Where are you going!?" John yelled back, "I don't know, I have all this energy!"

Ajh laughed, "Do not worry, he will be back, it is typical in young people." Shela said, "I know, I feel the urge to run myself. I feel good inside, real good! My body feels like its shaking! I am so glad we met you" and she gave Ajh a hug. Ajh said, "The shaking is the Holy Spirit, you will calm down in a while. John came back. He was out of breath and said, "I still feel like running, boy what a feeling! I would have never dreamt it would be like this!" Ajh asked, "Now who's crazy?" They all started laughing.

John looked at Ajh. "Are we going to receive robes too," with hesitation in his voice? They both looked at Ajh hoping he would say no. Ajh said smiling, "it is up to you, whatever you feel like wearing, but I think those clothes fit you for now." "Me too" answered John with relief in his voice, as they laughed. Ajh put his hands on their shoulders and said, "There are eyes watching us." They asked, "You mean God, Jesus, angels, who?" Ajh said, "the two little girls, Jennifer and Jasmine, they are up on the top of that small hill behind the bushes. They followed us here and have been watching." John said, "Those little rascals."

Shela asked, "They saw everything?" Ajh said, "Yes, the aura and the tongues of fire. God allowed them to see everything. It is good for young minds to see extraordinary things. It sparks and awakens areas in the mind that normally stay dormant. It is something lacking in your education today. You see those little girls, in a few years; will be growing strong in the word of God, doing healings, all kinds of miracles and spreading the word, while they are young. You two will help nurture this growth in them."

Ajh said, "I have to go now." Shela asked, "Where are you going and will we see you again?" Ajh smiled, "I am needed in another country and I will see you in Heaven. It is time to make myself more public. When you hear of me, there will be much controversy about the things I have said. Many will not believe, and I will not be accepted by religious people either."

"There will be someone else who will join me for several years. The words we speak will hurt many because it goes against people's way of life and beliefs. We will be hated. Then we will be shot to death and our bodies will lie in the sand for four days. Those that hate us, because of our words, will rejoice over our death. No one will touch our bodies, but on the fourth day the world will tremble. God will call us up and the world will see our bodies come to life and taken into Heaven. There will be a great earthquake and the beginning of sorrows. When all the scriptures are fulfilled, then you will see the coming of Christ out of the sky and the end of the world as we know it. Weep for those that have not prepared their souls, for they will be cast into the fire, and there will be weeping and gnashing of teeth. That is why you must save as many souls as you can before it is too late."

Shela asked, "Who is the other person?" Ajh answered, "I do not know. I will find out when it is time. While you are teaching, if people ask why does God allow so much pain and suffering and why is He punishing us? Tell them it is their own ignorance and lack of love for each other that has caused their pain and suffering. Tell them their brother, Satan, has fed these lies, knowing in their hearts of stone they will blame God. It is the path they have chosen. If they wish to be healed, all they have to do is ask, believe without doubt and have faith, and it will be done."

"If they ask you, why are we here, what is the purpose of life? Tell them, all of us want a purpose in life, and we feel lost and unfulfilled. These feeling are because you do not have God in your life. Seek His grace and blessings and keep your eyes fixed on Him. We are here for God's purpose to do his will, to enjoy the world as He created it. To allow God to live in our hearts and let Him experience the world through our senses. We are proof of His creativity. The closer you are to God, the closer you are to the truth."

"Tell them they are beings of light, energy and love, just as their Father in Heaven is a being of pure light, pure energy, pure love, and pure thought and they must return to the light to be whole. And that they are a channel for God's power and to use it to help others, as Jesus told you too. Do these things in the name of Jesus to give Him honor, and teach them the words of Jesus so they may know the truth and be saved. Because with out Jesus, we would be lost and confused. Jesus died, so we may be washed of our sins and He opened our eyes to God's ways. The words He spoke came from God, so they are true; you must learn the true meaning."

Tell them not to look upon each other as for the color of their skin, because this is only an outer shell that is discarded and turns to dust. But look at the spirit of each person, for everyone is your brother and sister, you should help each other grow toward God the Father."

"You must also baptize them with water saying, I baptize thee in the name of love, love of the Father who art in Heaven, love of Jesus Christ, our Savior, and love of the Holy Spirit, the gifts and essence of God. Amen. And those that show promise doing God's will and they follow in Jesus' footsteps, pray over them so they will be baptized of the Holy Spirit. And then they can be on their way with their own ministry."

"Teach everyone The Our Father, tell them too say this prayer before they ask God for blessings and everyday before you start your sermon. Where ever you go and no matter what language they speak you will understand them and they will understand you. The Holy Spirit will give you the knowledge. Sometimes someone speaks a language no one has heard before. This is what is called, speaking in tongues; it is a gift from the Holy Spirit."

"It is time. I must go now." He hugged them. "It has been a pleasure knowing and teaching you two" as he smiled, you could see the smile in his eyes also. Ajh backed up a few feet. Then he began to glow brighter and brighter. Shela and John turned their heads and covered their eyes, because the light was so intense, it was blinding. Suddenly the light was gone and so was Ajh. Shela and John looked at each other with sadness in their eyes. They were going to miss a brother they never knew they had.

Then they smiled and hugged each other. Shela said, "come on, we have work to do, spreading the word." They started to walk, then they stopped, turned around, John yelled out "come on girls, we see you." The two girls came out giggling and squealing with excitement. Their eyes wide open, chattering about what they saw. They were very excited. They all walked back to the houses with big smiles on their faces. The two girls talking a mile a minute ran ahead to tell Mama what they had seen.

Back at the house everyone was having a good time. They looked at Shela and John and could see something different about them. They were more radiant. And they all sang, danced and praised the Lord into the night.

The next day Mama started cooking, Shela and John began preaching. They stood with Mama for a long time. As the word spread of the healings, unlimited food for the poor, and listening to the word of God, every day more and more people came.

People set up tents and shacks, and settling down in the hills. They came from all over. Shela and John preached and healed people. Mama fed them. The people in the hills brought their instruments and made up songs of the Lord and helped Mama in the kitchen passing out food that God provided.

The old farmer found the path through the woods to the bottom of the gorge crossing a stream into the field of grass. He brought his cattle there and quickly multiplied his profits, so he gave a lot to charity. And supplied Mama with beef and chickens to feed the people. Every day the husband and wife would kneel and pray to God thanking Him for the blessings they received and for sending Ajh, Shela and John to save their souls.

People came and fixed Mama's house, gave it a new paint job inside and out. They fixed the wires, the porch and roof. A car dealer gave Mama a new car to get around in. But Mama hardly ever drove it; she was content being at home with the kids and the new lifestyle God provided. The donations bought new stoves, refrigerators and made more picnic tables, they even planted more trees for shade. Peter had some small construction equipment, so he fixed the road, going to Mama's house so it was passable and smoother, with the help of the people settling in the hills. The parents of Shela and John saw their picture in the newspaper as they became famous. So they came to see them and said how proud they were of them, and congratulated them on their marriage. Shela and John baptized their parents, as they stood there a while to listen to their children preaching the word of God, and watching the miracles they performed in the name of God.

After a while, Mama began preaching and healing, along with her two daughter's, Jennifer and Jasmine. While the woman in the hills cooked and prepared the food for the growing number of people. Jacob and Jackson grew tall and fine young men developing knowledge in constructing houses. They helped many of the people in the hills building and repairing their homes. Shela and John knew it was time to leave and to continue spreading the word of God. And they gave the Bibles that Ajh gave them to the two little girls.

Shela and John fasted for days to become closer to God and never made love since they were married. They knew a kind of love that very few people understand. Mama, the two girls, Shela, and John saved as many souls as they could, praising the Lord. Shela would often take the veil she kept from Ajh and look through it at John and say "you do get used to it." And Mama, at least once a week, made a small batch of burnt cookies and left them out on the picnic table with a glass of milk where Ajh sat, and by morning they were all gone. As for Ajh? Well, you will hear about him soon, very soon.

May God Bless You,
Love
Armand J. Horta

PUT ON YOUR ARMOR FOR GOD

Anchor your feet on the path toward the Father
Put on your armor of truth and righteousness
Put on your shield of God's Love
So Satan can not touch you
Open your heart of flesh to let God in
So you are full of love for everyone equally
Let your eye be single on the ways of God
And your body be filled with His Light
So you can not stumble in darkness
Let your tongue speak no evil or utter unkind words
Speak only that which comes from the mouth of God

Armand J. Horta

To those of you that are at war.

Do you not hear the words of God, when He says?
"Thou shalt not kill" and *"Love thy neighbor as thy self."*
All you are doing is fueling the problem. If you kill a child's mother or father, that child grows up with hatred in their heart.
Now terrorist groups and war lords always have new recruits.

If there are terrorist groups, or hate groups in your religion then you must openly denounce them and teach it is wrong, it is not of God. To those of you who join terrorist groups and war lords, is it not written in the scriptures, *"Vengeance is mine saith the Lord."* This goes for all religions because there are some religions that condone or say nothing against their parishioners who join hate groups who are against race or other religious beliefs. These people need education in the ways of God.

If you are easily persuaded by false religious leaders who say, if you kill the enemy you will be with God. Then you know nothing of God. If you break God's Laws then how can you go to Heaven?
Forgive your enemies, pray for those that persecute you. Hatred and a heart of stone and you will be cast into the eternal fire. For only with a heart of flesh will you enter Heaven. Have you not heard that the pen is mightier than the sword? Then every day write down words of God and your heart will be softened, you will be transformed and you will soon put down your weapons. The pen can change the world.

War is not the answer, only God the Father will give you the answer. If two countries that are in a dispute would pray to God, He will solve your problems. He will give you a sign. *"Ask and you shall receive."* If you do not strive for peace, then you are not of God. *"On Earth as it is in Heaven."*

Armand J. Horta

Here are some questions children asked about God.

When was He born?
God always existed, He is pure energy. Energy had to exist first in order to create matter. The opposite of what science believes.

How can He live for unlimited time?
God does not have limited time, because time does not affect spiritual beings. Time is only constant in the material world, and those who dwell on it so much.

What will it be like in the year 2012?
That depends if the people of Earth follow God we will see the world getting better, but we have a lot of praying to do. If we do not turn to God, things will progressively get worse. Everything we try to do will seem in vain. And a great fear will come over the people that do not believe in God.
A similar question asked. When will the world end? Only God knows, almost all of the scriptures have been fulfilled, but it will be delayed if everyone turns to God.

Why did Jesus die?
So the scriptures would be fulfilled about Him. He showed the world of His unending love for us, to bring us the truth about who we are and how to become a spiritual being. If He did not die, His life would have been lost in stories and today it would be thought of as a myth. But His blood washed us of our sins, we must take to heart His words and actions and follow Him. He showed us a path to God; we must become spiritual beings.

Why does God take our spirit to Heaven?
God does not take your life. We have a choice, and must decide on what path we wish to take. He takes your spirit when you have fulfilled your life on Earth. If you have lived your life by His Laws then you will be taken to Heaven.

Where do people go when they die?

They enter the spiritual world. Those who follow God's Laws and continually will go straight to Heaven. Others will go to different levels according to their deeds, until Judgment Day. Those who disrespect God and His Laws and do not show love and kindness toward everyone and to the creatures God created will go to hell.

How did God make all this?

God is unlimited Pure Energy and Pure Light. By rearranging the formula

$E=MC^2$ you can understand how to make unlimited matter. And at the speed of thought all God had to do is speak the word and matter was formed. Out of His breath is the energy of a thousand stars. Everything you see is made up of a form of energy. Even if you burn something it changes from one form of energy to another.

Can we sit in Heaven?

You can kneel, stand, sit and float what ever you want to do.

ABOUT THE AUTHOR

When I was born my grandmother Elizabeth told my parents I was going to be a priest. As a young boy in church looking at Jesus on the cross, I thought, what a terrible way for someone with so much love for us to die. The lettering on the cross INRI; to me it meant, In Rhode Island. Latter as an older teenager, I began to doubt my faith and became an atheist. I believed in Jesus that He was a good and intelligent man and was trying to show us how to achieve a higher form of existence. But I didn't believe that a being could create and control everything. I believed in life after death, my out of the body experience proved that the spirit can leave the body. I studied evolution and many subjects of science, even many subjects science didn't believe in, but there was always a missing link, which was God.

I was baptized by a friend, Frank Divozzi. Latter he told me when I opened the Bible to the Old Testament to be baptized, it meant that God The Father Himself choose me to be a reborn Christian. I started writing the book, but with the ups and downs and jobs working all hours', I didn't touch it for years. During those years I have witnessed, heard of, and been part of, many miracles and the wondrous things God has done. And how He has protected me from Satan's death grip many times, which are a few chapters in themselves.

About four years ago any church I went to the pastor would say; "God wants you to finish what you started," "you have many talents use them to help others," "your gifts are from God use them for His purpose." Every week these messages and more came and were aimed at me, my wife noticed it too. I knew it was time for me to finish the book.

The Holy Spirit of God blessed me with the ability to be able to pool information together to find answers. Where ever I would be I would pick up and read science books, magazines, newspaper articles of many subjects for over 38 years. I would find information I needed to know, sometimes just one paragraph out of an entire book or article. My hand opened the book, but God guided my hand.

ARMAND J. HORTA

BIBLIOGRAPHY

The HOLY BIBLE
(The Parallel Bible)
Containing the AUTHORIZED 1611 and
REVISED 1886 VERSIONS
Of the Old and New Testaments
A.J. HOLMAN & CO.
No. 1222 Arch Street, Philadelphia
1886

The words quoting the Bible came from this Bible and the sum of both versions. This Bible also contains the scholars and translators, artist sketches of cities and villages, Biblical scenery, coins, weapons, chronology of events and people and much more.

Also used;
Holy Bible
Reference Edition
King James Version
Copyright 1972 By Thomas Nelson Inc.
Regency Publishing House

The information about all other religions mentioned and their teachings:

The Worlds Great Religions
Life
Time Incorporated New York 1957

The section that mentions the Tibetan cave drawings comes from;
The Third Eye
By: T. Lobsang Rampa
Copyright 1956, 1958 by Brant & Brant

This edition published by arrangement with Doubleday & Company Inc.
Ballantine Books New York

The part in the book describing the crucifixion of Jesus comes from the Bible, information, and my interpretation. The description of one of the guards, that sharpened his dumbbell shaped metal pieces on his flagrum before whipping Jesus, and the information about the Shroud comes from the study of the Shroud of Turin. The book:

VERDIC ON THE SHROUD
By: Kenneth E. Stevenson and Gary R. Habermas
Banbury Books, Inc.
Dell Publishing Co., Inc.   1982

The information I spoke about the markings of the English alphabet and numbers 0-9 on butterflies and moths wings, was taken from a newspaper article in the Providence Journal- Bulletin, October 1, 1990 By C. Eugene Emery Jr. Journal-Bulletin Science Writer. The photographer was Kjell Sandved; he has been taking photographs of some 200,000 species around the world. And he found more images on their wings.

Like I said in the book, God put these designs so it would give mankind food for thought. He knew at a time when we are believing in evolution that we could travel the world and gather such information and it would prove that we came about by intelligent design.

I mentioned in the book about subliminal advertising, how corporations through the advertising media are manipulating people to buy their products, with sex, death, and now they use homosexual implications. Although I do not think this book is in publication, any longer you might be able to find an old copy;

SUBIMINAL SEDUCTION
By: Wilson Brian Key.
Penguin Group (USA) Inc.   Dec.1974

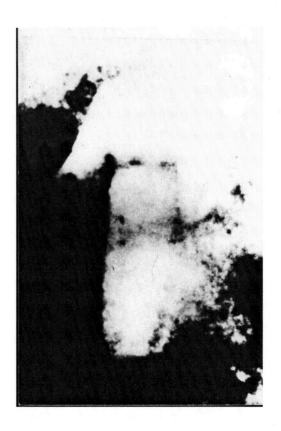

The Robe of Christ

I don't know where this picture came from, someone my wife worked with, and she made a copy of it. We have had it in our possession for over 15 years. The photographer is also unknown. The story is the photographer was in a plane and looked out the window into the clouds. As you can see, he saw the robe of Christ and took the picture.